OUTLINE

OF THE

PRINCIPLES OF HISTORY

(GRUNDRISS DER HISTORIK)

BY

JOHANN GUSTAV DROYSEN,

WITH A BIOGRAPHICAL SKETCH OF THE AUTHOR.

TRANSLATED BY

E. BENJAMIN ANDREWS,

New York · HOWARD FERTIG · 1967

907
D 790

First published in English in 1893

Howard Fertig, Inc. edition 1967

Library of Congress Catalog Card Number: 67-13644

PRINTED IN THE UNITED STATES OF AMERICA
BY NOBLE OFFSET PRINTERS, INC.

CONTENTS.

iii

TRANSLATOR'S PREFACE.

I BECAME interested in Professor Droysen as an historian so early as 1882. In real grasp upon the nature and meaning of history he seemed to me the superior of Ranke. This view I have not changed. To assist myself in comprehending his very deep thoughts I soon began a translation of the *Historik*. At first I had no idea of publishing, but as the value of the little work impressed me more and more deeply, I at last determined to English it for others. I subsequently laid the matter before Droysen, receiving his approval in the genial letter which appears upon a preceding page. I expected to finish the work in a few months from the date of this letter, but more pressing labors came and became permanent, so commanding my time that I have never since been able to devote to the translation more than now and then an hour. At last, however, after so many years, it is completed, and I give it to the public, appendices and all. These greatly elucidate the "Outline" proper, and may very appropriately be read first. Those who know Droysen's cumbrous yet nervous and abbreviated style of writing will not estimate the extent of my toil by the number of pages in this book.

Such was my reverence for Droysen that, after his death in 1884, I cherished the hope of preparing a

brief biography of him. I relinquished this half-formed
purpose partly for lack of time, and partly because
several excellent sketches of him presently appeared.
Max Duncker himself wrote two of these, one in Ivan
Müller's Biographical Year-Book for the Knowledge
of Antiquity, also published separately, and a more
extended one in the Prussian Year-Book for August,
1884 (LIV, *Heft* 2), edited by von Treitschke and Del-
brück. Duncker was Droysen's close friend, and had
access to much helpful material in manuscript. I in-
clined to translate one of his pieces for use in this
volume, but upon reflection thought the biography of
Dr. Hermann Krüger likely to be more interesting to
American readers. Professor G. Droysen, son of the
author of the "Outline," considers Krüger's account
on the whole better than aught else which was written
upon his father's life and work. This biography first
came out in the form of articles in the Mecklenburg
Anzeiger, the last one appearing on Saturday, August 2,
1884. Krüger, too, was an intimate friend of Droysen's. I could not have hoped to write anything better
than what these two competent and privileged biogra-
phers had presented. Besides, it was intimated to me
that Professor G. Droysen would sometime publish a
still ampler history of his distinguished father's life.

It is a reflection upon our times that such a man
as Droysen should so soon even seem to be forgotten.
I say this notwithstanding certain reasons for apathy
toward him grounded in the nature and habits of the
man. Owing to his intense application, and also to his
simple honesty, forbidding in him those arts by which
some German professors are popular, Droysen founded,

properly speaking, no school, though several of the German historians who earned fame during his last years and after his death were his pupils, inspired by his spirit and impressing upon their works the stamp of his manner. Among these may be mentioned Grünhagen, of Breslau, who has written so well on the first two Silesian Wars ; Reinhold Koser, of Berlin, who has edited several volumes of the Political Correspondence of Frederick the Great ; and S. Isaacsohn, author of the excellent *Geschichte des preussischen Beamtenthums.* Of these Koser is perhaps the ablest, though Grünhagen is famous for his fairness. In this he excels Droysen, who was often too controversial and always too favorable to Prussia. But not one of these younger historians so much as approaches the master in that wonderful wealth and control of materials exhibited by him in his *Geschichte der preussischen Politik.*

The " Outline " as it appears in English is in certain points somewhat more than a reflex of the original. In those paragraphs of Droysen's, and they are not few, which he so painfully abbreviated, leaving them hardly more than strings of catch-words for lecture-room amplification, the statements have been carefully pieced out into a fullness that will, it is hoped, give them clear meaning. For the Greek, Latin, French, and Italian with which the author loved to interlard his discourse, English has in most cases been substituted, the original being given either in brackets or in the margin. A few brief explanatory notes have been added at points where they seem most necessary.

I consider Droysen's *Historik* the weightiest book of its size composed in our century, weightier than any

other, small or great, save certain treatises by Hegel.
Yet I know the present tendency of historical study
too well to expect that all the English and American
historical scholars will read this book who, in my judgment, would greatly profit by reading it.   In most
directions one finds a stronger zeal for the knowledge
of history than for the understanding of history.   We
are so busy at gathering facts that no time is left us
to reflect upon their deeper meanings.   Too many
who wish to be considered historians seem hardly less
enthusiastic over the history of some town pump, provided it is "fresh" and "written from the sources,"
than over that of the rise of a constitution.   Happily
this fault is less pronounced than it was.   With increasing clearness is it seen that history is rationally interesting only as man's life is interesting, and that, touching
man's life, the element in which one may most legitimately feel deep interest is its moral evolution.   This
is emphatically Droysen's view, and in the " Outline "
he sets it forth in a more inspiring and convincing
manner than is done by any other writer whom it has
been my privilege to read.   May this translation enable
many to derive from his profound conceptions even
more profit than they have brought me.

E. BENJ. ANDREWS.

Brown University,
      September 6, 1892.

AUTHOR'S PREFACE.

LECTURES upon the Encyclopedia and Methodology of History which I delivered from time to time, beginning with 1857, led me to write out the skeleton of the same in order to give my auditors a basis for my oral amplification. In this way, as manuscript, first in 1858 and then again in 1862, the following "Outline" was printed. Numerous requests, some of them from foreign lands, determined me, when the little volume had to be printed anew, to give it to the public. Hindrances and scruples of many kinds have delayed the publication until now, when at last, according to my provisional judgment at any rate, the work is ripe.

To the first impression, in order to give a general idea of the questions discussed in the body of the work, I had prefixed an introduction. This still stands at the beginning. A couple of articles are appended to the treatise, which will, I trust, serve to illustrate certain points touched therein. The first, entitled "The Elevation of History to the Rank of a Science," was occasioned by the appearance of Buckle's well-known work, and printed in von Sybel's "*Zeitschrift*" for 1852. The second, on "Nature and History," was evoked by a discussion in which all the advantages of the metaphysical point of view were on my opponent's side. In the third article, under the title of "Art and Method," I have collected what is hardly more than a succession of aphoristic remarks, intended to bring to memory the partly forgotten limits between dilletantism and science. Some of them have already found place in an academic lecture. See the *Monatsberichte* of the Royal Academy of Sciences, July 4th, 1867. I hesitated whether or not to add a fourth discussion, some copies of which I had printed as an introduction to the second part of my " History of Hellenism " in 1843. I wished on the basis of this to investigate with scientific friends precisely this problem of the principles of history, a problem from which the point of view between theology and philology held by me in the History of Hellenism and branches of learning related thereto, seemed to me to derive justification. This discussion I have preferred to postpone, because it appeared unlikely that readers would be as much interested as myself in knowing the point whence I set out and the roads I traveled to reach the conclusions presented in the following pages. The purpose of this publication will be attained if it serves to incite further inquiry into the questions which it treats, touching the nature and task of History, its method and its competency.

BERLIN, November, 1867.

PREFACE TO THE THIRD EDITION.

In this new impression of the "Outline" the arrangement has been in some points altered, into a form which repeated delivery of the lectures indicated as better answering my purpose. In the somewhat numerous paragraphs which have double figures,[1] those in brackets refer to the order in the editions of 1867 and 1875.

The "Outline" itself makes it clear that it does not pretend to be a "Philosophy of History," and also why it does not look for the essence of History in that which has opened so splendid a career to natural science.

JOH. GUST. DROYSEN.

Berlin, July 18, 1881.

---

[1] Not reproduced in this translation. — *Tr.*

BIOGRAPHICAL SKETCH.

JOHANN GUSTAV DROYSEN.

By Dr. Hermann Krüger.

On the morning of June 19, 1884, in the Villa at Schöneberg, near Berlin, whither he had removed upon medical advice, died Johann Gustav Droysen, in whom Germany lost one of its best men and one of its greatest historians. To the author of these lines, a grateful pupil of his, it is no less a necessity of the heart than a duty of piety to lay a crown of honor upon this man's grave.

Let us begin by briefly sketching the outward course of Droysen's life.

Born on the 6th of July, 1808, at Treptow, on the Rega, as son of a minister, and early left an orphan, he obtained his preparation for the university at the *Marienstift-Gymnasium* in Stettin. He then studied philology in Berlin, and obtained there his first position as teacher, in the Gymnasium of the Gray Cloister. In 1833, having already published some studies in the domain of Greek history, he habilitated as privat-docent at the Berlin University, where he delivered philological and historical lectures with great acceptance, and also advanced very soon to the position of professor extraordinary. In 1840 he accepted a call to become ordinary (full) professor of history in the University of Kiel, where he worked with great success till 1851. At the same time he took an influential part as a politician

in the agitations to which during the forties the popula-
tion of Schleswig-Holstein had recourse in view of
Denmark's threat to take possession of these duchies by
force. In 1848 Droysen was sent from Kiel by the
provisional government of the duchies as their repre-
sentative to the Diet of the Confederation, and later
as deputy to the German National Assembly.

In the year 1851 Droysen was called to the University
of Jena, to which he belonged as one of its first
ornaments through the eight following years. From
there he accepted in 1859 a call to the University of
Berlin, where he had begun his academic career, and
where from this time on for another quarter century
he wrought with a success which was great and which
continued to the last. His lectures were among the
most frequented at the university. Particularly those
upon modern history drew together in his auditorium,
besides numerous students, also many high civil and
military officers and many *savans*. For Droysen was
not merely an eminent savant and historical investigator,
but also an extraordinary teacher.

As savant and historian he published, from every one
of the universities to which he successively belonged,
one or more works which have exalted his name as
among the most brilliant in the scientific world.

To his first Berlin period belongs the translation of
Æschylus that appeared in 1832, which Droysen, —
as a young philologist, also as an enthusiast for
the most powerful among the Greek dramatists, —
undertook at first in the interest of a friend not
adequately acquainted with the Greek, and only subsequently gave to the press. His appreciation of the

Greek nature, his poetic endowment, and his unusual mastery of the speech, begot by their union a translation which stands forth masterful in its kind and has not been surpassed even to this day. To be sure, the philologists of 'strict observance' most violently attacked this free poetic imitation, which is true rather to the spirit and thoughts of the writer than to the letter. But Droysen was not drawn astray. Convinced that he who will bring a Greek poet like Æschylus or Aristophanes pleasurably to the understanding of a German reader must utterly renounce the literal mode of rendering, he immediately followed with his translation of Aristophanes. This, like that of Æschylus, speedily found the favor of the public and has kept it even to our own days.

Both translations, on which Droysen, as is proved by the rendering of certain verses and the change of various expressions, has been working right along, exist now in third editions. What power they have to afford high satisfaction and delight even to the most rigid philologists, the writer of these lines learned when, during his time in Leipzig, he listened to the exposition of the Knights of Aristophanes by Ritschl, and more than once heard that eminent critic express his admiring approval of Droysen's version.

Meantime there unfolded itself in Droysen, side by side with his philological genius, still more emphatically the talent and the inclination for historical investigation and exposition; and having once pressed his way into the sphere of Hellenic things, he saw in the thorough investigation of Grecian antiquity the principal task of his scientific calling. A fruit of these Hellenic studies was the History of Hellenism, begun in Berlin, finished later in Kiel, to which work of several volumes the History of Alexander the Great serves in a way as introduction. 'It is,' says the author in his preface, 'a highly significant yet almost forgotten development of political and national relations which we have endeavored to fathom and expound.' The result was a satisfactory presentation of an epoch till then little known, yet highly important, — wherein, amid the violent and often confused struggles of Alexander's generals and successors, those *diadochi* and *epigoni*, the Greek spirit was brought into connection with the Oriental nature, so as, by a process of fermentation, decomposition, and illumination, to cause a mighty transformation in the thinking and feeling of the ancient world, by which, withal, the path was leveled for Christianity. Droysen apprehends his problem from elevated points of view and solves it, bringing clearness into the tangled chaos of overpowering material, with undeniably great dexterity. Leo, in his Universal History, names this work 'an excellent treatment of the subject.' Upon this, too, however, sharp attacks were not wanting, and they were partly well founded. For Droysen, still at that time a thorough Hegelian, had in his handling of the epoch allowed quite too much play to the Hegelian method of constructing history, thus thrusting much, particularly respecting Alexander and his plans, into incorrect perspective and false lights. Subsequently he saw this himself, and in the preface to the second edition of this work, with the perfect honor peculiar to his character, he confessed his error.

Here in Kiel, where Droysen completed his remarkable work, the History of Hellenism, he completed also
his transition from ancient to modern history.   In 1846
he published his lectures on the History of the Wars
for Freedom.   In an ingenious manner, with an almost
perfect art of luminous construction and rich coloring
in his presentation, such as he equaled nowhere else in
his works, that period so excessively abounding in
struggles, transformations, developments, and results, is
unfolded and depicted in speech that is fresh, resonant,
often out and out ravishing.   Whoever wishes a per-
fectly clear consciousness of the difference between
the born and schooled historian and the *dilettante*, should
compare this History of the Wars for Freedom, which for
a long time has not in our judgment been sufficiently
appreciated, with Beitske's much lauded work upon
the same period.   Although in many parts left behind
by more recent investigations, this work of Droysen's
still presents such a fullness of spirited remarks and
incisive historical observations, that the perusal of it
even affords genuine enjoyment.

A second work which Droysen begun at Kiel but
finished later in Jena, was the famous Biography of
Field Marshal York of Wartenburg, at present in its
ninth edition.   To say anything at so late a day in
praise of this book, which in its classic completeness
stands forth simply unique in biographical literature,
would be carrying owls to Athens.   We will only
remark that although the occasion for the composition
of the book was an outward one, Droysen nevertheless
seized upon it with joy, in the conviction that in that
lax period of peace nothing was better adapted to

strengthen the people's patriotic and moral consciousness than the example of a great personality like York,
energetic, yet ruled by the most rigid sense of duty.
The portrayal of this hero's character was especially
intended to be an example to strengthen in the simple
service of duty the young Prussian army, exposed in
its long and often tedious garrison life to the danger of
laxity.

It was in the time of deep political excitement
and exhaustion which naturally followed the stirring
period of the later forties, when Droysen began his
labors at Jena.   A condition of almost entire discouragement had come in as to the vigorous reconstruction of
Germany.   The national dreams, wishes and strivings
lay upon the ground like a sea of blossoms.   Droysen
understood this general despair but did not share it.   It
was his irrefragable conviction that although this first
attempt to erect the German Empire again had failed,
it would be followed by others, and that at last, provided Prussia would only, in proper recognition of her
historical calling, brace herself up to an energetic policy,
the loosely connected German states would unite under
her lead into a firm whole, and thus realize after all the
perpetual dream of a new German Empire.

Borne on by this firm hope and conviction, Droysen
began his colossal work, the History of Prussian Policy,
the first volume appearing in 1855.   In this path-breaking work, which furnishes evidence no less of the
author's unwearied lust for toil than of his prodigious
power for toil, Droysen introduces us into the history
of the origin of the Prussian state, and shows how this
state, amid perpetual struggles with inner and outer

difficulties, with labor most intense and efforts often in vain, in ever new, energetic onsets, toiled its way up, furthered and utilized all the powers necessary for the subsistence and prosperity of the modern state, so as at last to enter, a German state with full credentials, into the rank of Europe's great powers. A prodigious plenitude of material from the archives was for the first time wrought into form and published in this work. In consequence, many views previously accepted as certain have been given up, some facts placed in new lights, and much else brought to the day as absolutely new.

However, this epoch-making work, which we peruse now in thirteen thick volumes, will hardly prove popular in the sense in which Mommsen's Roman History, for instance, or Ranke's History of the Reformation, has become so. Such a result is prevented not only by the great compass of the treatise but more than all by the circumstance that it does not present a history of the Prussian state, embracing and unfolding in richly colored view the entire breadth and manifoldness of the state's life, but simply, as the title says, a history of Prussia's 'policy,' to follow out which in its progressive realization of exalted ideals is for one not an historian often wearying.

We may regret that Droysen did not choose to write a comprehensive history of the Prussian state ; we may blame him for falling, in this work too, here and there, though less frequently than before, into the Hegelian habit of historical construction ; yet the History of Prussian Policy remains forever a standard treatise, path-breaking, foundation-laying, epoch-making. No subsequent historian having to explore the same domain, will be permitted with impunity to slight Droysen's labors. That the author was awarded for it by the scientific commission appointed to make the award, the great prize of a thousand Thalers founded by Frederick William IV, to be given every five years for the best historical work appearing during the same, was only the proper recognition of the astonishing industry, great critical acumen and scientific thoroughness characterizing the elaboration of this work; a work which insures Droysen for all time the glory of being reckoned among Germany's most remarkable historians. It ends, at present, with the account of the first two Silesian wars. On the basis of private information which has come to me to the effect that the remainder was found in his desk ready for the press, quietly and peacefully closed, as what he wished to give to the public, we may cherish the hope that a fourteenth volume will follow, bringing us to the beginning of the Seven Years' War.[1]

Droysen has been not only an historical investigator especially favored of heaven, but also a preëminently remarkable teacher of history. He brought great inborn talent to the teacher's calling; yet this would perhaps not have attained so full activity had he not learned before his entrance upon his academic career, namely as teacher at the Gray Cloister, to exercise and develop this talent practically in minor relations. This first period of teaching was a decided advantage to him in his entire later activity as university instructor.

---

[1] This has since been published, and reaches to the opening of the Seven Years' War. — *Tr.*

Masterly was Droysen's knack of grouping his historical material in his lectures so as to render it visible
clearly and visible all together, and of maintaining the
essentials thereof in harmonious relation with minor
historical details.   The matter did not press itself
upon the attention in a too massive manner, nor on the
other hand was it swamped by historical observations.
In his portrayal of given epochs, in his characterization
of towering personalities, in his definite grasp of leading points of view, he possessed the art of a great
master.   Yet to go further and portray historical personalities in their outward manifestation, as Ranke
loves to do and does in such a brilliant manner, Droysen
invariably refused.   'Whether any one has yellow hair
and blue eyes,' he once said derisively, 'is a question
on which nothing depends ; in devoting attention to
that sort of thing an historian descends to miniature
painting.'   It would certainly have been welcome to
many of his hearers and readers if he had not so
completely renounced this means of concrete representation.

Droysen held you spell-bound in his lectures, which
moved upon the middle line between free utterance
and literal delivery from manuscript.   He did this by
his splendid diction, by his sharp and ingenious exposition, by his extraordinary art of letting, at the right time
and place and often only by a brief, hint-like remark, a
surprising blaze of light flash upon special personalities.   Great also was the effect of the powerful, manly
spirit which got expression in all these ways.

Hence Droysen's lectures could not but convoke
a great company of listeners.   They did this even to

his last days, although other and younger lights with
equally great power of attraction later arose at his side
as colleagues.   To hear Droysen was, as one often heard
said, a delight, and for the sake of this delight many of
his hearers neglected taking notes.   Yet any one who,
like the undersigned, in spite of the great temptation
merely to listen, consistently practiced taking notes,
knows how durable and precious a treasure he possesses
in a *Heft* written down from Droysen's deliverances.

But what so permanently chained his pupils and
made them hearken to their teacher's words, almost as
if in worship, and what drew them always again
straight to his lectures, was at bottom, if I see rightly,
Droysen's peculiar, mighty personality, which, with its
powerful tendency to the ideal, had its roots deep in the
moral.   Such a personality ever exercises upon academic
youth, so susceptible to the ideal, an irresistible magical
effect, not to be undervalued.   For the best that a
teacher who is, besides, an ethical personality, can give
to his pupils, is and remains in the last analysis,
himself.   This is as true in a certain sense of the
university teacher as of any.   Droysen was a personality
full of high moral earnestness, and he always energet-
ically asserted even in his lectures the point of view
of the moral judgment.   'The moral,' so he expressed
himself on one occasion, 'is that which constitutes every
man's final worth, that is, his only worth.'   How much
sympathy he has therefore (compare the first volume of
the History of Prussian Policy) with Henry VII, of
Luxemburg, and how little for the talented Talleyrand
in his utter frivolousness !   Not rich talent, or preëminent
genius with its egoistic tendency, but unselfish sur-

render to the idea of the good, he viewed as alone
worthy of respect and admiration. 'What,' he once
asked, 'is the truly great in history? It is controlled,
ennobled, glorified passion'; but yet, so it reads further
in his Principles of History, 'everything historically
great is only a sun-mist in the manifestation of God.'

Not in the sphere of the Greek world — as people
have supposed, and as Hans Prutz has again recently
asserted and emphasized in the *National-Zeitung* — not
in the sphere of the Greek world did Droysen's moral
view of the universe have its roots, but in the soil of
Christianity. In his thought the development of
humanity — whose preparatory stages he characterizes as
recognition of self and recognition of the world (see his
Principles of History) — completes itself in the recognition of God. History itself is to him 'not the light and
the truth but only a witness and a conservation of them,
a sermon upon them; as John was not himself the Light
but sent to bear witness of the Light.' The warmth
and luminousness of this deep moral view streamed out
through his lectures, although it was not Droysen's
manner to repeat or to express it in definitely formu-
lated utterances or propositions.

During his exuberant activity Droysen delivered over
two hundred courses of lectures, before assemblies
always numerous, of academic youth. They embraced
as well ancient as modern and the most recent history.
Besides, he lectured over and over again upon the
Encyclopedia and Methodology of History. This
course presented an infinite abundance of instructive
and inspiring matter, and, in the opinion of the undersigned, was for the prospective historian simply

indispensable. Perhaps not too strong was the recent assertion that it is doubtful whether a course like that of Droysen's on the Encyclopedia of History will ever be delivered again by any university teacher.

Many placed his course of lectures on Greek history at the head. This certainly combined Droysen's comprehensive knowledge of the ancient world with his deep understanding of Greek affairs, his sympathetically reproductive sense for Greek thinking and action, and for the changing forms of Greek political life and of Greek national art, in such wise as to render it a highly interesting and instructive course. What Droysen presented was not mere dry information, that pains had hunted up and collected; but, supported by the thorough and many-sided knowledge that he had won by long years of study, he reconstructed from the fullness of his living vision the Greek world in its political and social development, in its aspects of light and shade, in its rise and its decadence.

Years after, there came back to me a vivid recollection of those lectures. I was temporarily residing in Berlin and was taking a walk with Droysen in the *Thiergarten* one fine August evening. It was, if I mistake not, in the summer of 1877. Our conversation led to the contests of the *diadochi*, and from these back to Alexander and Demosthenes. Knowing Droysen's derogatory judgment of the statesman Demosthenes, I found it easy by an utterance of a contrary tenor to evoke his contradiction and to lead him on to a fundamental justification of his view. In speech that was all life and motion Droysen now not only unfolded in the most various directions an astonishing abundance of ready information, but swept forwards and backwards, with so deep a grasp of Greek relations, that a wish more lively than ever came over my soul : Oh that this man had chosen to think out a Greek history for us ! Oh that he in preference to so many others had been called to fill up this painful gap so long felt !

Still larger than Droysen's classes in ancient history were those which heard him upon modern and the most recent periods. The lectures upon the latter were of even more universal interest than the others. In them he took his hearers from about the middle of the fifteenth century on to the fifties of the present century, setting down and maintaining as landmarks to his separate but continuous lectures the Thirty Years' War, the Seven Years' War, the Wars for Freedom, and the Revolutionary time of 1848 with its proximate results. These lectures bore, like the others, a thoroughly spirited, inspiring and at the same time strongly scientific character ; but they had an incomparably greater practical effect upon the immediate present, many securing through the deeper understanding which these lectures afforded of German history, a better insight into the present and its tasks, so that the power of the political shibboleth, which especially in the first half of the sixties dominated so much the musings and aspirations of our youth, was more and more broken.

It is equally true that Droysen extremely seldom allowed himself, near as the temptation often lay, an allusion to present political revolutions, and when he did indulge it was done in a brief and definite word. Thus, once, in the winter of 1864, when the constitu-

tional conflict was at its height, he closed a lecture with
these words : 'It was the curse of this party that it,
precisely like our party of progress to-day, ended by
placing party-interest above interest in the Fatherland.'
In consequence of this concluding utterance, his entire
academic audience, which was then in great part feeling
the touch of progressist breath, became excited.   The
students determined, against the next evening, should
Droysen in his customary brief recapitulation again be
guilty of a remark so deeply injurious to progressist
feelings, to raise the cry of 'scandal' and to make an
infernal racket.   Apprised of this plot, Droysen came
on the following evening into the large auditorium,
this time full even to suffocation, ascended the platform
with easy step, and, glancing over the assembly with a
firm look out of his large dark eyes, began : 'We concluded yesterday evening, gentlemen, with the words':
and then followed exactly the final words of the preceding lecture.   All was silent ; not a person stirred.
Every one had the feeling that he who stood upon that
platform was a *man*.

As in his lectures, Droysen's special talent for teaching showed itself also in the historical society con-
ducted by him, whose members assembled around him
every Saturday in his study.   The reading of the paper
that had been prepared on the assigned theme was
followed by a debate, Droysen leading, in which he, in
a fashion open and free yet of extreme forbearance,
criticised what had been presented, and thereby set
forth the method of historical investigation in a manner
at once thorough and inspiring.   His efforts progress-
ively to form his pupils to scientific, independent

investigations and undertakings, had great and enduring support in his ability quietly and surely to find
his way into every one's individuality.

During the time of conflict in the sixties, when,
among others, his colleague, Herr von Sybel, fought
boldly in the ranks of the then party of progress against
Bismarck and the Prussian government, Droysen declined participation by speech or writing, and only occa-
sionally indicated his position, which was not that of the
opposition. Subsequently, too, when those great events
and transformations leading to the erection of the
national state were taking place, he greeted them
rather with silent joy than with loud acclaim, and, in
general, the older he grew, he held himself more and
more aloof from the political contests of the day, in
order by silence and solitude to live more entirely in
his scientific labors.

Yet Droysen, too, had his time in which duty and
conscience seemed to command him to come forward
publicly with a manly word. It was during his period
of labor at Kiel. The decrees of the provisional
estates-assembly held at Roeskild in the year 1844,
threatened the rights of the duchies, Schleswig and
Holstein, and would have been dangerous had the
Danish crown followed them. These acts called
Droysen into the political arena. He composed what
has become celebrated as the ' Kiel Address,' which met
with a storm of approval and was instantly covered
with thousands of subscriptions. As in this writing,
so subsequently, in a second, namely when Frederick
VII announced the consolidated-constitution of Denmark, Droysen came out with noble manliness, and

glowing through and through with patriotic wrath, in opposition to Danish arrogance. 'What business,' a passage of it reads, 'has Denmark with us? What we with Denmark? We have no mind for any price whatever to be guilty of treason to ourselves and to Germany.' 'Heed,' he further warns the Danes, 'heed the evolving time. Disdain ye what we have spoken, fill ye the king's ear with adverse counsel and your heart with the unrighteous plunder;[1] then see to it what sort of advice ye are giving yourselves! We are the wards of a great people, a great Fatherland.'

Droysen's intervention in this patriotic way for the cause of the duchies in those evil days, his accurate knowledge of the relations in question, and his sharp political vision, specially qualified him to represent the cause of the duchies elsewhere as well. He was therefore sent by the provisional government subsequently established, as its confidential agent to the Diet of the Germanic Confederation at Frankfort. When, then, in consequence of that movement which shook Germany in the spring of 1848, the National Assembly convened at Frankfort, Droysen was chosen to this also. He joined the so-called hereditary-imperial party, and, as member of the committee on the constitution, drew up its protocol. Afterwards, when men's hope-filled dreams of a new, united Germany had melted like snow, Droysen, with Dahlmann, E. M. Arndt and others, in May 1849, left the National Assembly.

'Pale as a corpse,' so Droysen once told the story in after years, 'Dahlmann entered the hall in order to set his name to the notification of departure. All eyes

[1] 'Geliebt.'

were upon him. Deeply moved and scarcely master of himself, he seized the pen and subscribed. What he suffered was for him notification of the death of all his patriotic hopes.' Droysen was less destitute of courage, though he, too, was bowed to the very earth. Even in those most evil days he could not and would not let go the hope of a renewal of the German Empire. Henceforth, as before, he placed his entire reliance on Prussia, whose calling to advance to the pinnacle of a newly united Fatherland he viewed as irrefutably demonstrated by her history.

As an historian he conceived to be equally certain his duty to stamp this historical calling of Prussia fast and deep upon the soul of the despairing race of his days — a promise, as it were, of a better future. He accordingly began that work of his, planned in the broadest style, the History of Prussian Policy. In this he now espied the principal task of his life, and to it he henceforth consecrated his entire strength.

After his service at Frankfort Droysen never again came forward as member of a political body. It was, we have already remarked, not without hope in his heart that he bade farewell to Frankfort. He had looked upon the business of the first German parliament as simply a first, though unsuccessful effort, to be followed by others with happier result; and in the album provided for its members — characteristically enough of his then view of things — he wrote, slightly altering the Vergilian verse : *Tantae molis erat Germanam condere gentem!* But he would not again accept a commission to public political activity, and he declined with emphasis an election to the parliament at Erfurt. 'Any one who has made such a fiasco as we did at Frankfort,' he expressed himself on a later occasion in his open, honest way, 'ought to give these things once for all a wide berth and relegate them to other and more artful hands.'

However, in his scientific labors and in pushing forward his masterpiece, he continually nourished his own hope and that of his nation. And when the mighty events of the year 1866 announced the break of a new day, and in the autumn of that year the author of these lines again visited him at his home, almost his first words, spoken with joyful confidence, were, 'Now the movement will go through and what we have been so long striving for will succeed.' A few years more and he saw his prediction, boldly spoken in a time of discouragement, that the Hohenzollern would sometime take the place of the Hohenstauffen, fulfilled to the letter. The splendor of the Empire, fresh from its resurrection, glorified the evening of his declining life.

Droysen's nature had the build of genius. His ability was many-sided. To a sharp, deeply penetrating intellect he joined a lively, mobile imagination, along with a fine feeling for form and a decided sense for the realities of life and for their worth. His poetic sensibility, which qualified him beyond many others for the translation of an Aeschylus and an Aristophanes, did not hinder him from becoming and remaining, as a pupil of Boeckh's, likewise a philologist in the best sense of the word. Full as he was of ideal elevation, it was not in the circle of thoughts prevalent in the Hellenic world, whose deep shadows he recognized beyond almost every other historian, but in the real sphere of Christianity, that he found full and enduring satisfaction for the

moral need of his nature.   Once an enthusiastic pupil
of Hegel, he later became a thorough connoisseur and
admirer of Aristotle.   Indeed, a decided inclination to
philosophic thinking formed a strongly prominent feature
of his character.   To the end of his days Droysen
applied himself to philosophical studies with a persist-
ence and a thoroughness hard to be matched by any
modern historian, although the results of this are not
immediately manifest in his writings, unless we take
into account his tendency, which increased with his
years, toward abstract expressions.

Amid this abundance of richest endowment Droysen did not dissipate his power, but with the unusual energy characteristic of him, was able to limit
himself to the realm for which it was manifest he was
peculiarly adapted, that of history.   A master in investigating details, as is shown by his minor but thoroughly
classical treatises upon Pufendorf, Eberhard Windeck,
the Marchioness of Bayreuth, the Strahlendorf Opinion,
and others, he was at the same time an historical
investigator on a larger scale, who never in viewing the
particular lost from his eye its connection with the
great whole.   His innate drawing to Universal History
led him to cultivate departments farthest removed from
one another, the world of antiquity no less than that of
the closing Middle Age and modern times.   Yet these
different periods appeared to him not as disconnected
fragments, but as an historic totality organically united.
This susceptibility of his for universal history, as well
as the sharpness and thoroughness with which he
investigated, and equally with these the great variety
of his scientific works, assure to Droysen for all time

his place among the *Coryphœi* of German historians, putting him among moderns in immediate connection with Ranke.   And he is, indeed, so far as I have observed, as yet the only historian whom any one, as Professor Maurenbrecher essayed to do in discussion some years ago — has ventured to compare with Ranke.

The relation between these two great historians, who for years worked side by side at the same university, was unfortunately not the best.   The causes of this may here so much the better be left unexplained, in that the undersigned, to tell the truth, is unable clearly to assign the ultimate reason for the phenomenon. Meanwhile let us all the more rejoice — remembering a word from Goethe — in the fact that we can call two such men with their mighty creations forever 'our own.' The aged Ranke still[1] works away with the strength of youth upon his Universal History, for whose completion all adherents and admirers of this great historian heartily wish him undiminished mental as well as bodily freshness.   Droysen, some thirteen years younger, to the great pain of his numerous pupils and reverers, is much earlier than many expected removed from temporal scenes.   With a constitution tender on the whole, Droysen long ago felt his power declining, and nothing but the great energy with which he bore up in spite of increasingly morbid conditions made it possible for him to continue his lectures till just before last Whitsuntide.   Even three days before this festival he delivered in his customary manner his carefully elaborated paper in the Academy of Sciences, a member of which he had been for years.

[1] July, 1884.   Ranke died on May 23, 1886.

Only a little while before his end, upon the pressing advice of his physician, he saw himself necessitated to announce by a notice upon the blackboard a cessation of his lectures for that Semester. He was destined never to resume them. His strength sank rapidly. His children hurried anxiously to his side, to ease by their devoted and loving care the last days of their father, who since the death of his dearly loved second wife had been alone. Meantime his weakness increased, unconsciousness alternating with consciousness. Once more, however, four days before his end, Droysen's strong love for work came back. He had himself carried to his writing-desk and his pen handed him. But the fingers that had so often guided it now refused the service. Deeply moved, Droysen laid down the pen, tears streaming from his eyes. He knew it now; he was at the goal. He proceeded to arrange everything with care, even in respect to his funeral. On the evening of June 18th the shadows of death sank down around him deeper and deeper. But yet, clear to the last, he had for every tender service of love, bringing its brief alleviation, its transient coolness to the heated head, a mild, friendly smile of thanks. Thus, surrounded by the faithful, ministering love of his children, he fell softly and calmly asleep.

Wind and clouds now play over the spot which conceals what of Droysen was mortal; but the breath of immortality also sighs above that grave and sweeps withal through the works which he created.

Have, pia anima.

DR. HERM. KRÜGER.

BOLTENHAGEN, July, 1884.

OUTLINE

THE PRINCIPLES OF HISTORY.

Outline of the Principles of History.

———•◦•———

No one will withhold from historical studies the recognition of having, like others, their place in the living scientific movement of our age. New historical discoveries are busily making, old beliefs are examined afresh, and the results presented in appropriate form.

But if we demand a scientific *raison d' être* for these studies, if we wish to know their relation to other forms of human knowledge, and the underlying reason why they take the course they do, they are not in condition to give satisfactory information.

Not that they regard themselves logically above such questions, or incompetent to solve them. Now and then an attempt has been made to do this, the solution having been sometimes put forward within the very circle of historical studies, sometimes borrowed from other branches of learning. By some the history of the world is assigned a place in the Encyclopedia of Philosophy. Writers of a different tendency, skeptical about logical necessities, all the more confidently on this account recommend us to develop history out of material conditions, out of the figures put down in statistics. Another, and he only expresses in the form of a theory what men without number are thinking or have thought, questions the very existence of 'so-called history.' 'Peoples exist purely in the abstract; the individual is the real thing. The history of the world is strictly a mere accidental configuration, destitute of metaphysical significance.' Elsewhere, pious zeal — pious, of course, more in appearance than in reality, insists upon substituting the miraculous workings of God's power under his unsearchable decree, for the natural causal connection of human things, a doctrine having this advantage, at least, that, being stated, it is under no further indebtedness to the understanding.

Within the sphere of historical studies, even so early as the close of the Eighteenth Century, the Göttingen school of that day had busied itself with these general questions ; and they have been handled afresh from time to time ever since. Writers have undertaken to show that history is 'essentially political history,' and that the many sorts of elementary, auxiliary and other sciences belonging to our department group themselves around this kernel. Then the essence of history has been recognized as consisting in method, and this characterized as a 'criticism of the sources,' as a setting forth of the 'pure fact.' Others have found the definitive task of our science in artistic exposition, 'the work of the historical artist,' and even celebrate as the greatest historian of our time him whose exposition approaches nearest to Sir Walter Scott's romances.

The historical sense is too active in human nature not to have been forced to find its expression early, and, wherever conditions were fortunate, in appropriate forms ; and it is this natural tact which points out the way and gives the form to our studies even at the present time. But the pretensions of the science could not be satisfied with this. It must make clear to itself its aims, its means, its foundations. Only thus can it exalt itself to the height of its task ; only thus, to use expressions from Bacon, can it set aside the preconceptions now governing its procedure, the idols of the theatre, tribe, forum and den, for whose maintenance just as powerful interests are active now as once interposed in favor of astrology, of lawsuits against witches, and of belief in pious and impious witchcraft. By thus becoming conscious, history will make good its jurisdiction over an incomparably wider realm of human interests than it is likely or possible that the science should master otherwise.

The need of attaining clear conceptions touching our science and its problem, every instructor who has to introduce youth into the study will feel, just as I have, though others will have found out how to satisfy it in a different manner. I for my part was urged to such investigations especially by a sort of questions which are usually passed over because in our daily experience they seem to have been solved long ago.

The political events of to-day, to-morrow belong to history. The business transaction of to-day, if of consequence enough, takes rank after a generation, as a piece of history. How is it that these mere affairs turn into history?[1] What criterion is to determine whether they become history or not? The contract of purchase concluded to-day between private individuals, — is it the thousand years that transforms it into an historical document?

Every one declares history to be an important means of culture ; and in the education of to-day it certainly

[1] *Geschäfte* into *Geschichte*.

is a weighty element. But why is it thus? In what form? Did not history render the same service to the Greeks of the age of Pericles? To be sure the form was different then, — probably that of the Homeric Songs. And how can national poems have had to Greeks and to Germany under the Hohenstauffen the educational value of historical instruction?

Observation of the present teaches us how, from different points of view, every matter of fact is differently apprehended, described and connected with others; how every transaction in private as well as in public life receives explanations of the most various kinds. A man who judges carefully will find it difficult to gather out of the plenitude of utterances so different, even a moderately safe and permanent picture of what has been done and of what has been purposed. Will the correct judgment be any more certain to be found after a hundred years, out of the so soon lessened mass of materials? Does criticism of the sources lead to anything more than the reproduction of views once held? Does it lead to the 'pure fact?'

And if such querying is possible as to the 'objective' content of history, what becomes of historical truth? Can history be in any sense characterized by truth without being correct? Are those right who speak of history in general as a fable agreed upon? A certain natural feeling, as well as the undoubting and agreeing judgment of all times tells us that it is not so, that there is in human things a unity, a truth, a might, which, the greater and more mysterious it is, so much the more challenges the mind to fathom it and to get acquainted with it.

Right here another list of questions presented itself, questions touching the relation of this potency in history to the individual, touching his position between this and the moral potencies which bear him on and bring him to self-realization, touching his duties and his highest duty; considerations leading far beyond the immediate compass of our study, and of course, convincing us that the problem by them presented was to be investigated only in its most general connections. Could one venture to undertake such investigation with only the circle of information and attainments that grow out of the historian's studies? Could these studies presume, as the studies of nature have done with so splendid a result, to make themselves their own foundation? One thing was clear: that if the historian, with his merely historical cognizance of what philosophy, theology, the observation of nature, etc., have wrought out, was to take hold of these difficult problems, he must have no inclination to speculate, but must in his own empirical way proceed from the simple and solid basis of what has been done and discovered.

I found in William von Humboldt's investigations the thought which, so I believed, opened the way to a sort of a solution to these problems. He seemed to me to be for the historical sciences a Bacon. We cannot speak of a philosophical system of Humboldt's, but what the ancient expression ascribes to the greatest of historians, 'political understanding and the power of interpretation,'[1] these he possessed in remarkable harmony. His thinking, his investigations, likewise the

[1] ἡ σύνεσις πολιτικὴ καὶ ἡ δύναμις ἑρμηνευτική.

wonderful knowledge of the world won through that active life of his, led him to a view of the world which had its centre of gravity in his own strong and thoroughly cultivated sense of the ethical. As he traced out the practical and the ideal creations of the human race, languages in particular, he became acquainted with the at once spiritual and sensuous nature of the race, as well as with the perpetually creative power which, as men mutually impart and receive, belongs to the expression of this nature;. these, the nature and the power, being the two elements in which the moral world, producing, so to speak, ever new electric currents in ever new polarizations, moves by creating forms and creates forms by moving.

It appeared to me possible by the aid of these thoughts to pierce deeper into the question of our science, to explain its problem and its procedure, and, from a true recognition of its nature, to develop in a general way its proper form.

In the following paragraphs I have endeavored to do this. They have grown out of lectures delivered by me upon the Encyclopedia and Methodology of History. My aim has been to give in this "Outline" a general view of the whole subject, and to hint at particulars only so far as seemed necessary to make clear the sense and connection.

INTRODUCTION.

———◦◇◦———

I. — HISTORY.

§ 1.

Nature and History are the widest conceptions under which the human mind apprehends the world of phenomena. And it apprehends them thus, according to the intuitions of time and space, which present themselves to it as, in order to comprehend them, it analyzes for itself in its own way the restless movement of shifting phenomena.

Objectively, phenomena do not separate themselves according to space and time ; it is our apprehension that thus distinguishes them, according as they appear to relate themselves more to space or to time.

The conceptions of time and space increase in definiteness and content in the measure in which the side-by-side character of that which is and the successive character of that which has become, are perceived, investigated and understood.

§ 2.

The restless movement in the world of phenomena causes us to apprehend things as in a constant development, this transition on the part of some seeming merely to repeat itself periodically, in case of others to supplement the repetition with ascent, addition, ceaseless growth, the system continually making, so to speak, 'a contribution to itself.'[1]   In those phenomena in which we discover an advance of this kind, we take the successive character, the element of time, as the determining thing.   These we grasp and bring together as History.

§ 3.

To the human eye, only what pertains to man appears to partake of this constant upward and onward motion, and of this, such motion appears to be the essence and the business.   The *ensemble* of this restless progress upward is the moral world.   Only to this does the expression 'History' find its full application.

§ 4.

The science of History is the result of empirical perception, experience and investigation, ἰστορία.   All empirical knowledge depends upon the 'specific energy' of the nerves of sense, through the excitation of which the mind receives, not 'images' but signs of things without, which signs this excitation has brought before it.   Thus it develops for itself systems of signs, in which the corresponding external things present themselves to it, constituting a world of ideas.   In these the mind, continually correcting, enlarging and building up *its* world, finds itself in possession of the external world, that is, so far as it can and must possess this in order to grasp it, and, by knowledge, will and formative power, rule it.

---

[1] ἐπίδοσις εἰς αὐτό.   Aristotle, *de anima*, II, 5, 7.   Appendix II at the end of this "Outline" is an amplification of §§ 1 and 2 here.

§ 5.

All empirical investigation governs itself according to the data to which it is directed, and it can only direct itself to such data as are immediately present to it and susceptible of being cognized through the senses. The data for historical investigation are not past things, for these have disappeared, but things which are still present here and now, whether recollections of what was done, or remnants of things that have existed and of events that have occurred.

§ 6.

Every point in the present is one which has come to be. That which it was and the manner whereby it came to be, — these have passed away. Still, ideally, its past character is yet present in it. Only ideally, however, as faded traces and suppressed gleams. Apart from knowledge these are as if they existed not. Only searching vision, the insight of investigation, is able to resuscitate them to a new life, and thus cause light to shine back into the empty darkness of the past. Yet what becomes clear is not past events as past. These exist no longer. It is so much of those past things as still abides in the now and the here. These quickened traces of past things stand to us in the stead of their originals, mentally constituting the 'present' of those originals.

The finite mind possesses only the now and the here. But it enlarges for itself this poverty-stricken narrowness of its existence, forward by means of its willing and its hopes, backward through the fullness of

its memories.   Thus, ideally locking together in itself
both the future and the past, it possesses an experience
analogous to eternity.   The mind illuminates its
present with the vision and knowledge of past events,
which yet have neither existence nor duration save in
and through the mind itself.   'Memory, that mother of
Muses, who shapes all things,'[1] creates for it the forms
and the materials for a world which is in the truest
sense the mind's own.

§ 7.

It is only the traces which *man* has left, only what
man's hand and man's mind has touched, formed,
stamped, that thus lights up before us afresh.   As he
goes on fixing imprints and creating form and order, in
every such utterance the human being brings into
existence an expression of his individual nature, of his
'I.'   Whatever residue of such human expressions and
imprints is anywise, anywhere, present to us, that
speaks to us and we can understand it.

II. — THE HISTORICAL METHOD.

§ 8.

The method of historical investigation is determined
by the morphological character of its material.   The
essence of historical method is *understanding* by means
of *investigation*.

§ 9.

The possibility of this understanding arises from the
kinship of our nature with that of the utterances lying

---

[1] μνήμην ἁπάντων μουσομήτορ' ἐργάνην. — Æschylus, *Prometheus*, 460.

before us as historical material. A further condition of this possibility is the fact that man's nature, at once sensuous and spiritual, speaks forth every one of its inner processes in some form apprehensible by the senses, mirrors these inner processes, indeed, in every utterance. On being perceived, the utterance, by projecting itself into the inner experience of the percipient, calls forth the same inner process. Thus, on hearing the cry of anguish we have a sense of the anguish felt by him who cries. Animals, plants and the things of the inorganic world are understood by us only in part, only in a certain way, in certain relations, namely those wherein these things seem to us to correspond to categories of our thinking. Those things have for us no individual, at least no personal, existence. Inasmuch as we seize and understand them only in the relations named, we do not scruple to set them at naught as to their individual existences, to dismember and destroy them, to use and consume them. With human beings, on the other hand, with human utterances and creations, we have and feel that we have an essential kinship and reciprocity of nature : every 'I' enclosed in itself, yet each in its utterances disclosing itself to every other.

§ 10.

The individual utterance is understood as a simple speaking forth of the inner nature, involving possibility of inference backward to that inner nature. This inner nature, offering this utterance in the way of a specimen, is understood as a central force, in itself one and the same, yet declaring its nature in this single voice, as in every one of its external efforts and expressions. The individual is understood in the total, and the total from the individual.

The person who understands, because he, like him whom he has to understand, is an 'I,' a totality in himself, fills out for himself the other's totality from the individual utterance and the individual utterance from the other's totality. The process of understanding is as truly synthetic as analytic, as truly inductive as deductive.

§ 11.

From the logical mechanism of the understanding process there is to be distinguished the act of the faculty of understanding. This act results, under the conditions above explained, as an immediate intuition, wherein soul blends with soul, creatively, after the manner of conception in coïtion.

§ 12.

The human being is, in essential nature, a totality in himself, but realizes this character only in understanding others and being understood by them, in the moral partnerships of family, people, state, religion, etc.

The individual is only relatively a totality. He understands and is understood only as a specimen and expression of the partnerships whose member he is and in whose essence and development he has part, himself being but an expression of this essence and development.

The combined influence of times, peoples, states, religions, etc., is only a sort of an expression of the absolute totality, whose reality we instinctively surmise and believe in because it comes before us in our ' *Cogito ergo sum*,' that is, as the certainty of our own personal being, and as the most indubitable fact which we can know.

§ 13.

The false alternative between the materialistic and the idealistic view of the world reconciles itself in the historical, namely in the view to which the moral world leads us ; for the essence of the moral world resides in the fact that in it at every moment the contrast spoken of reconciles itself in order to its own renewal, renews itself in order to its own reconciliation.

§ 14.

According to the objects and according to the nature of human thinking, the three possible scientific methods are : the speculative, philosophically or theologically, the physical, and the historical. Their essence is to find out, to explain, to understand. Hence the old canon of the sciences : Logic, Physics, Ethics, which are not three ways to one goal, but the three sides of a prism, through which the human eye, if it will, may, in colored reflection, catch foregleams of the eternal light whose direct splendor it would not be able to bear.

§ 15.

The moral world, ceaselessly moved by many ends, and finally, so we instinctively surmise and believe, by the supreme end, is in a state of restless development and of internal elevation and growth, 'on and on, as man eternalizes himself.'[1] Considered in the successive character of these its movements the moral world pre-

---

[1] *Ad ora ad ora come l'uom s'eterna.* — Dante, *Inferno*, XV, 84.

sents itself to us as History. With every advancing
step in this development and growth, the historical
understanding becomes wider and deeper. History,
that is, is better understood and itself understands
better. The knowledge of History is History itself.
Restlessly working on, it cannot but deepen its investigations and broaden its circle of vision.

Historical things have their truth in the moral forces,
as natural things have theirs in the natural 'laws,'
mechanical, physical, chemical, etc. Historical things
are the perpetual actualization of these moral forces.
To *think* historically, means to see their truth in the
actualities resulting from that moral energy.

III.—THE PROBLEM OF THIS "OUTLINE."

§ 16.

This *Historik* or discussion of the Principles of
History is not an encyclopedia of the historical sciences,
or a philosophy or theology of history, or a physics of
the historical world. Least of all is it a discipline for
the artistic composition of history. It must set its own
problem, which is to be an organon of historical thinking
and investigation.

§ 17.

Canvass the history of this problem from Thucydides
and Polybius to Jean Bodin and Lessing. The kernel of
the question is in William von Humboldt's *Introduction
to the Kawi-language*. See also Gervinus's 'Principles
of History' [*Historik*], Comte's 'Positive Philosophy,'
Schäffle's 'Structure and Life of the Social Body,' etc.

§ 18.

'Historik' embraces three doctrines : that of method for historical investigation, that of the system belonging to the matter to be historically investigated, and that of the systematic presentation of the historical results.

THE DOCTRINE OF METHOD.

§ 19.

Historical investigation presupposes the reflection that even the content of our 'I' is a mediated content, one that has been developed, that is, is an historical result (§ 12.) The recognized means of this mediation is memory, ἀνάμνησις. Our knowledge is at first a something received, a something which has passed over to us, ours, yet as if not ours. It is a long step to where we feel ourselves free with this knowledge, and have it freely at our command. Out of the totality of that which we thus fully possess, out of *our* appreciation of this 'content' as ours, and our recognition of ourselves in it, there is begotten in us (§ 10) a new idea of this knowledge as a whole, of each part of it and of each particular element in it. This idea arises in us involuntarily. There it is as a matter of fact. But is the truth really as this idea presents it to us? To be convinced touching its validity we must reflect upon the manner in which it had origin in us; we must investigate the combination of means through which we come by it; we must test it, make it clear, prove it.

I. — INVENTION.

§ 20.

The point of departure in investigation is historical interrogation. Invention puts us in possession of the materials for historical work. It is the miner's art, that of finding and bringing to the light, 'the underground work.'[1]

§ 21.

Historical material is partly what is still immediately present, hailing from the times which we are seeking to understand (Remains), partly whatever ideas human beings have obtained of those times, and transmitted to be remembered (Sources), partly things wherein both these forms of material are combined (Monuments).

§ 22.

Amid the abundance of historical Remains may be distinguished :

(*a*) Works whose form is due to human agency, — artistic, technical etc., as roads, plats of leveled ground, and the like.

(*b*) Conditions constituting what we have spoken of as the 'moral partnerships,' viz., customs and usages, laws, political and ecclesiastical ordinances, and the like.

(*c*) Whatever sets forth thoughts, items of knowledge, or intellectual processes of any kind, as philosophemes, literatures, mythological beliefs, etc., also historical works as products of their time.

[1] Niebuhr.

(*d*) Papers relating to business, as correspondence, business bills, archives of all sorts, and other things of this nature.

§ 23.

Remains in the creation of which the purpose of serving the memory coöperated with other aims, such as ornaments, practical utility, etc., are Monuments. These include documents to certify to posterity when a piece of work was concluded, likewise all kinds of works of art, inscriptions, medals, and in a certain sense, coins. Finally comes in every kind of marking by means of monuments, even the stone landmark, and things as insignificant as titles, arms, and names.

§ 24.

Under Sources belong past events as human understanding has apprehended them, shaped them to itself and passed them over to the service of the memory.

Every recollection of the past, so long as it is not externally fixed, as in verses, in sacred formulæ, or in written composition of some kind, partakes the life and the transformation of the circle of ideas belonging to those who cherish it. Tradition in the Church of Rome illustrates this. The credibility of oral tradition is only quantitatively different from that of written.

Our Sources may grasp the subject either in a predominantly subjective way, or in the closest possible accord with the facts, 'pragmatically.' To the subjective order belong partly such Sources as present a view clouded by a superabundance of phantasy or of feeling, like legends, historical lyrics, etc., partly such as use historical matter of fact only as material for considerations and arguments of a different nature, as speeches in court, parliament, etc., documents relating to public law, etc. The Prophets, Dante, Aristophanes, etc., also illustrate Sources of this kind.

Within the 'pragmatic' order of Sources we may distinguish those which mostly impart only isolated facts, from those which classify more. In addition to this difference the aim with which the facts were apprehended will help to determine the meaning of our Sources. The apprehension will obviously vary according as it was intended to aid the author's own memory, or for others, for one person, or a few, or all, for contemporaries or for posterity, for instruction, for entertainment, or for purposes of business.

The so-called 'Derived Sources' are views of other men's views.

§ 25.

The three species of materials will vary in relative value according to the purpose for which the investigator is to use them. Even the very best give him, so to speak, only polarized light. By the use of what we have termed Remains, he may with entire certainty penetrate to minor data, yes, even to the very minutest. The keener his sight in fathoming these deeps the more will he get out of them. However, data of this class form but accidental and scattered fragments.

In consequence of the nature of its materials empirical inquiry in history must dispense with the great helps which corresponding study in the physical world possesses in observation and experiment. Still the fact that all sorts of experiments are yet making in the moral world and under the most thorough observation, compensates historical investigation through the clearing up of its obscure 'x' by means of analogies.

§ 26.

Historical Interrogation results in our ascertaining what Remains, Monuments and Sources are to be brought forward for the 'reply.' It is the art of historical 'investigation' to extend and complete the historical material; and especially: (*a*) by search and discovery, as of a diviner; (*b*) by combination, which, putting things in their proper places, makes into material for history that which appears not to be such: witness A. Kirchoff's History of the Greek alphabet; (*c*) by analogy, which casts light upon the subject through similarities of result under similar conditions; (*d*) by hypothesis, proof of which is evidence for the event in question. The last would be illustrated by the level ground plats of the ancient German villages as expressions of order in the primitive community.

§ 27.

'Invention,' like each of the parts of Historical Method yet to be named, presupposes the continual coöperation of the others. For every one of them all historical knowledge and all other related knowledge, whether philological or pertaining to general facts, serves as an auxiliary science.

II. — CRITICISM.

§ 28.

Criticism does not seek 'the exact historical fact'; for every so-called historical fact, apart from the means leading thereto, and the connections, conditions and purposes which were active at the same time, is a complex of acts of will, often many, helping and hindering, and acts of will which, as such, passed away with the time to which they belonged, and lie before us now only either in the remnants of contemporary and related transformations and occurrences, or as made known in the views and recollections of men.

§ 29.

The task of Criticism is to determine what relation the material still before us bears to the acts of will whereof it testifies. The forms of the criticism are determined by the relation which the material to be investigated bears to those acts of will which gave it shape.

§ 30.

(*a*) We must inquire whether the material actually is what it is taken to be or pretends to be. Reply to this question is given by 'criticism of its genuineness.' Proof of ungenuineness is complete when the time, the origin or the aim of the falsification is proved. The thing so proved ungenuine may serve in some other direction as weighty historical material.

One application of the criticism of genuineness in reference to a given department is Diplomatics. The business of this branch is the testing of the genuineness of records and other pieces of writing by outward signs, in contrast with the so-called 'higher criticism.'

§ 31.

(*b*) We must also inquire whether the material has maintained its original and pretended character unchanged, or, if not, what changes are to be recognized as having occurred in it and as therefore to be left out of account. This question is answered in the 'criticism of earlier and later forms,' known as 'diacritical procedure.' This procedure usually results in the pointing out of a so-called 'development' from the first form to the form before us. In such a demonstration the separated parts are mutually explanatory and confirmatory [Ferdinand Christian Baur].

§ 32.

(c) We must inquire, still further, whether the material, under the circumstances of its origin, did or could involve all that for which it is, or offers itself to be, taken as voucher; or whether, immediately at that time and place, it must not have been, or may not even have proposed to be, correct only partially, relatively and in a certain way. This question finds answer in the 'criticism of correctness or validity.'

This form of criticism must ask :

(1) Whether, judged by human experience, the fact stated is in itself possible.

(2) Whether it is possible considering the alleged conditions and circumstances.

In both these cases the criticism measures, in reference to the objects or events in question, both the given view itself and also the correctness of this view.

(3) Whether any beclouding of vision is recognizable in the motives, aims or personal relations of the author of the account.

(4) Whether incorrectness was unavoidable through insufficiency of the means for observation and forming judgment.

In each of these cases, (3) and (4), criticism gauges both the view arrived at and its correctness, in the light of the process and of the instrumentality by which the view was arrived at.

§ 33.

The application of the criticism of correctness to Sources is technically called 'Source-criticism.' If this is understood only in the sense of pointing out how one author has used another, it is only an occasional means, one among others, its business being to present or prepare demonstration of correctness or incorrectness.

The Criticism of Sources distinguishes :

(1) What a given source-document has grasped, reproduced, and now presents, as events, transactions, original words, earlier sources, etc.

(2) What general coloring this source-document received from the circle of ideas prevalent at the time and place of its origin, for instance the 'demonological' coloring of the fifteenth century, or the *ennui*, as of *epigoni*, characterizing the Alexandrian period.

(3) What individual complexion the author himself has in virtue of his culture, his character, some special tendency, or the like.

§ 34

The primitive 'source' does not consist in the dreary maze of contemporary opinions, accounts, reports. This is only the daily repeated atmospheric process of ascending and self-precipitating vapors from which the true Sources or springs are replenished.

As a rule the earliest historical composition respecting an event governs all subsequent tradition. That case is the most fortunate where this composition is contemporary with the events which it handles; that is, before the effects produced by events have brought any change of view concerning the efficient facts and persons, and before any new, epoch-making event has created a different world of thought.

§ 35.

(*a*) We must inquire whether the material as we have it still contains all the points for which the investigation seeks testimony, or in what measure it is incomplete. This question finds answer in the critical arrangement of the verified material.

Always, or nearly always, we have before us only single points out of the facts as they originally were ; only individual views of what existed and occurred. Any historical material has gaps in it, and even the most exact investigation is not free from errors. The measure of sharpness wherewith these gaps and possible errors are signalized is the measure of the certainty of our investigation.

The critical arrangement is not settled merely according to the point of view of succession in time, as with annals. The more manifold the points of view from which the same materials are arranged, the larger is the number of solid points which the intersecting lines will afford. The registers in the *Corpus Inscriptionum Latinarum* illustrate this.

§ 36.

The outcome of criticism is not 'the exact historical fact.' It is the placing of the material in such a con-

dition as renders possible a relatively safe and correct
view. The conscientiousness which refuses to go
beyond the immediate results of criticism, makes the
mistake of resigning all further work with these results
to fancy, instead of going on to find such rules for this
further work as shall assure its correctness.

III. — INTERPRETATION.

§ 37.

Beginnings are neither sought by criticism nor demanded by interpretation. In the moral world nothing
is without medial antecedents. Yet historical investigation does not propose to explain, in the sense of
deriving, as mere effects and developments, the latter
from the earlier, or phenomena from laws. If the
logical necessity of the later lay in the earlier, then,
instead of the moral world, there would be something
analogous to eternal matter and the changes of matter.
Were the life of History only a reproduction of what
is permanently identical with itself, it would be void of
freedom and responsibility, without moral content and
only of an organic nature. The essence of interpretation lies in seeing realities in past events, realities with
that certain plenitude of conditions which they must
have had in order that they might become realities.

§ 38.

As in walking are united (*a*) the mechanism of the
moving limbs, (*b*) the tension of the muscles according
to the evenness or unevenness, smoothness, hardness,
etc., of the ground, (*c*) the will which moves the body,

and (*d*) the purpose which leads the person who wills
to walk, so criticism completes itself from four points
of view.   The exaltation of any one of these as by
itself essentially or exclusively determinative of validity, is the source of many theoretical and practical
errors.   It is doctrinaire (§ 92).

§ 39.

(*a*) ' Pragmatic ' interpretation takes up the body of
criticised facts according to the causal nexus naturally
binding together the original events in their course, in
order to re-construct this course of events as it once
actually was.   By ' body of criticised facts ' is meant
those remains and those views of the once actual course
of events which have been verified and arranged in the
work of criticism.   In case of plentiful material the
simple demonstrative procedure is sufficient.   If the
material is defective, the nature of the thing as made
known to us from similar cases leads us to apply
analogy, viz., a comparison between the known quantity
and the ' x ' in question.   The analogy between the
two ' x's ' so far as they are mutually supplementary,
yields the ' comparative procedure.'   The supposition
of a connection in which the matter possessed by us
only in fragments displays itself as fitting into the
' curve ' of the assumed connection, thus confirming
itself visibly, as it were, is ' hypothesis.'

§ 40.

(*b*) The ' interpretation of the conditions ' proceeds
upon the truth that we must think the conditions which
made the original fact possible and possible so and so,

as a part of the fact itself, and hence as certain to
enter, however fragmentarily, into all views and remnants of the fact. Thus the position, in itself not
beautiful, of the Borghese gladiator reveals the line of
the pediment for which the statue was intended.

The conditions relating to space, omitting innumer-
able insignificant ones, receive elucidation from details
like the geography of a theatre of war and of a battle-
field, the position of a country's natural boundaries,
the valley formation of Egypt, the marshes upon the
North Sea, and many more.

The conditions of time comprise that already present
state of things into which the event in question made
its entry, and the contemporary events which had a
more or less determinative effect upon it.

A third order of conditions is found in the means,
material and moral, by which the course of things was
rendered possible and actual. The material means include the manifold sorts of substances and instruments,
and along with these an immeasurable field of 'technological interpretation,' which thus far remains almost
untouched. The moral means include the passions of
men, the moods of the masses, the prejudices or views
governing them, etc. The general, the statesman, the
artist, who wishes to operate upon the masses and
through them, has his character in that same measure
determined by them.

§ 41.

(c) 'Psychological interpretation' seeks in the
given fact, the acts of will which produced it. Such
interpretation may take cognizance of the subject who
willed, and of the energy of his volition so far as this

influenced the course of events under survey, and of his intellectual force so far as this determined his will. But neither did the subject of the volition fully exhaust himself in this one turn of things, nor did that which came to pass come to pass merely through the strength of this one man's will or intelligence. It is neither the pure nor the entire expression of his personality.

Personality as such does not find in History the tests of its value, in what it undertakes, does or suffers there. To it is reserved a circle of its own, wherein, however poor or rich in gifts it may be, significant or insignificant in respect to effects or results, it has to do with itself and its God, a circle of its own, wherein is the truest source of its willing and existence, where that takes place which justifies or condemns it before itself and before God. His conscience (*Gewissen*) is the most certain (*gewisseste*) thing which the individual possesses ; it is the truth of his existence. Into this sanctuary the ken of investigation does not press.

Human being understands human being, but only in an external way; each perceives the other's act, speech, mien, yet always only this one deed or feature, this single element. Prove that I understand my fellow rightly or entirely I cannot. It is another thing for a friend to believe in his friend ; or, in a case of love, for the one party to hold fast to the other's image as that other's true self : ' Thou must be so for so I understand thee.' That sort of confidence is the secret of all education.

The poets, as Shakspere, develop the course of events which they present, from the characters of certain

persons. They poetize on to each event a psychological
interpretation.   But   in   actual   facts   effects   come
through   other   elements   than   personalities.   Things
take   their   course   in spite   of   the   will,   good   or   bad, of
those   through   whom   they   come   to   pass.   The   continuity   of   History,   its   work   and   its   advance,   lies in the
moral   potencies   (§ 15).   In   these   potencies   all   have
part,   each   in   his   place.   Through   them,   mediately,
even   the   meanest   and   poorest   participates   in   the   life of
History.   But   even   the   most   highly   endowed   man,
strongest   of   will   and   most   exalted   in   power,   is   only an
element   in   this   movement   of   the   moral   potencies,
though   always,   in   his   place,   specially   characteristic   and
efficient.   In   this   *rôle*   and   in   this   only   does   historical
investigation   view   any   man,   not   for   his   person's   sake
but   on   account   of   his   position   or   work   in   this   or   that
one   among   the   moral   potencies,   on   account   of   the   idea
whose   bearer   he   was.

§ 42.

(*d*)   The 'interpretation of ideas' fills   up   the   gap
which   psychological   interpretation   leaves.   For   the
individual   builds   a world   for   himself   in   that   measure
in   which   he   has   part   in   the   moral   potencies.   And   the
more   diligently   and   successfully   he   builds,   in   his   place
and   for   the   brief   space   of   his   life,   the   more   has   he
furthered   those   partnerships   in   which   he   lived   and
which   lived   in   him;   and   the   more   has   he   on   his   part
served   the   moral   potencies   which   survive   him.   Without   them   man   were   not   man;   but   they   develop,   grow
and   rise   only   in   the   united   work   of   men,   of   peoples,   of
times,   only   in   the   progressive   history   whose   development   and   growth   is   their   unfolding.

The ethical 'system' of any period is only the grasping and bringing together of the ethical life thus far unfolded; only an attempt to sum it up and speak it out according to its theoretical content.

Every period is a complex of the outworkings of all the moral potencies, however developed or rudimentary their unfolding may be, however much the higher may still be veiled in the lower, as when the State existed in the form of the family.

§ 43.

In the great diversity of the moral spheres wherein human life takes root and moves, investigation finds the list of questions with which it approaches any given historical material in order to interpret it as to its ethical content.

We can proceed in either of two ways.

(a) We may take a statical view, observing in the materials before us the state of the moral formations as they existed at the time in question and up to that time. In this way we get the 'ethical horizon' within which stood everything that was and was done at this period among this people. We thus secure the measure for every individual process within this period among this people.

(b) Or, dynamically, we may seek and seize the progressive elements in the given state of moral formations, and by putting these into relation with that state to which they have led in acting themselves out, catch sight of the movement at that period and among that people, the striving and struggling of men, their victories and defeats.

§ **44**.

In such movement it is now this, now that, among the moral potencies, which takes the lead, and it often seems as if this leading potency were alone involved, everything else being subordinate to it. As the thought of this time, this people, this man, it inflames men's minds and leads, dominates and impels society to take a step essentially forward.

The thought or the complex of thoughts which interpretation points out in any course of events, is to us the truth of that course of events. The course of events is to us the effect, the phenomenal form, of this thought.

Our methodical reproduction of the facts must by its correctness enable the thought to make good its character as underlying the course of events, and the course of events to justify the thought. For that thought is to us true to which an existence corresponds, and that existence true which corresponds to a thought.

THE DOCTRINE OF SYSTEM.

§ **45**.

The realm of historical method is the cosmos of the moral world. The moral world as it sweeps restlessly on from past to future every moment forms an endless maze of affairs, circumstances, interests, and conflicts. There are manifold points of view, technical, legal, religious, political, and the like, from which this moral scene can be considered and scientifically handled.

What goes on daily in this moral world is never done or purposed by any sensible person as history. It is only subsequently that a peculiar way of surveying the finished and the past makes history out of common doings (*Geschichte* out of *Geschäfte*). To apprehend the moral world historically means to apprehend it according to its development and growth, according to the causal succession of its movement (§ 15).

§ 46.

The secret of all movement or motion is its end (τὸ ὅθεν ἡ κίνησις). Inasmuch as historical investigation is directed to the advancing movement of the moral world, takes account of its direction, sees end after end unveil and fulfil itself, it infers and concludes (§ 12) to a supreme end wherein the movement completes itself, wherein what makes this world of men keep moving, circling and ceaselessly hastening on is seen to be rest, consummation, an eternal present.

§ 47.

The human being during his space of life in the finite has, in virtue of his likeness to God, to be an infinite subject, a totality in himself, his own measure and end ; but not being like the Godhead also a *causa sui*, he has not to become, unaided, what he ought to be. Into his character as a human being he develops only in the moral partnerships. The moral potencies form him (§ 12). They live in him and he lives in them. Born into an already existent moral world — for the first child had father and mother — thus born to be conscious, free and responsible, each man for himself (§ 42) in these moral partnerships and using them as helps, builds his little world, the bee-cell of his 'I.' Each of these cells is conditioned and supported by its neighbor, and in turn conditions and supports. All together they form a restlessly growing building, conditioned and supported by the existence of its minute, yes, of its minutest parts.

§ 48.

By this building and forming process in its individuals, developing as it works, humanity creates the cosmos of the moral world. Without the restless growth and development of its moral partnerships, that is, without History, its work would be like a mountain of infusoria shells. Without the consciousness of continuity, viz., without History, its work would be as barren as a plain of sand, the sport of the winds. Without the consciousness of ends and of the highest end, without the Theodicy of History, its continuity would be a mere motion in a circle, repeating itself.

§ 49.

The moral world is to be considered historically :

I. In relation to the Matter wherein it creates forms.

II. In relation to the Forms into which it shapes itself.

III. In relation to the Workers through whom it builds itself up.

IV. In relation to the Ends which realize themselves in its movement.

I. — THE WORK OF HISTORY IN RELATION TO ITS KINDS OF MATTER.

§ 50.

The Matter for the work of History comprises what nature originally gave and what History itself has evolved. Both these are at once the condition and the means of this work, at once its business and its limitation. The ceaseless enlargement of the matter for the work is the measure of the enlargement of the work itself.

§ 51.

(*a*) As man studies and comprehends *nature*, rules and transforms nature to serve human ends, the work of History lifts nature up into the moral sphere, and spreads abroad over the circle of the earth the signs, the *aerugo nobilis* of human will and power. Such signs are discoveries, inventions, improvements, agriculture, mining, the training and breeding of animals, changes produced in countries and landscapes by the transmigration of plants and animals, the circle of the sciences, and many others parallel to each of those named.

§ 52.

(*b*) The work of History causes the mere creature man, by discovering in the sweat of his brow what he is designed to be, to realize this design and to discover it by realizing it. Out of the mere *genus homo* it thus makes the historical man, which means the moral man. Amplification of this would involve Anthropology,

Ethnography, the question of races and of the crossing of races, the propagation of the human race, and so on.

§ 53.

(*c*) Those human formations which have come to be, resulting from the work and circumstances of History, are constantly becoming in their turn norm to that work, as well as impulse and means to new work. Hence the value of statistics. Hence the historian must study poverty, commerce, etc., and all that comprises the so-called history of civilization.

§ 54.

(*d*) Out of the purposes of men and the ardor or passion with which they surrender to these, History forms her incentives and impelling forces, and produces her massive effects. National spirit, particularism, fanaticism, rivalries and so on illustrate this.

II. — THE WORK OF HISTORY IN RELATION TO ITS FORMS.

§ 55.

The Forms in which the work of History moves on are the moral partnerships, whose types, as moral potencies, are in the heart and conscience of human beings. 'He who cannot enter into community or who on account of his self-sufficiency needs nothing, is either a brute or a God.'[1] In the moral potencies lies the

---

[1] Ὁ δὲ μὴ δυνάμενος κοινωνεῖν ἢ μηδὲν δεόμενος δι' αὐτάρκειαν . . . ἢ θηρίον ἢ θεός ἐστι. — Aristotle, *Politics* I, 1, 12.

educating might of History, and every one has part in the life of History in the measure in which he has part in them (§ 41). Human relations are moral in the measure in which they educate; and they educate in the measure in which the moral element in them is mighty.

Each of these moral potencies creates its sphere, its world for itself, shut up in itself, and yet making the demand on every man to come forward with it and labor on its behalf, at the same time setting in activity and working out in it his own moral worth.

The individual is not an atom of humanity, one of the molecules which laid together in infinite number would produce humanity. He belongs to his family, people, state, etc., is a living member only through them, 'as the hand separate from the body is no longer a hand.'

The doctrine of native human rights goes beyond its own premises. It forgets that there is no right without duty, and that a thousand kinds of obligations are fulfilled toward every individual before he himself has been able to acquire a right.

§ 56.

The partnerships, in accordance with the nature of the human being, spring either from a natural need, or from an ideal one, or partly from each. As moral potencies they have a development and a history as well in themselves as in relation to other potencies and to everything else.

§ 57.

A. In the 'natural partnerships' that which is natural has to be made moral by means of a primary process of will, by means of love, fidelity, duty etc. The fact that among men a partnership of soul issues from a natural need, and from mere impulse a life of volition and obligation and a permanent bond, distinguishes the human being from the lower creatures.

§ 58.

(*a*) THE FAMILY. — Here, in the narrowest space, in the forms lowest down towards the creature, are found the strongest moral ties, the deepest social substructures. Under this rubric consider, with much else, the gradations of marriage up to monogamy, paternal authority, the family hearth, so-called patriarchal government, and blood-vengeance.

§ 59.

(*b*) THE NEIGHBORHOOD. — Here come into view the first developments of friction in the spatial collocation of men, involving the foundation of the village community as a great family. Consider the elders, the constituency of the community, the various plots of land.

§ 60.

(*c*) THE TRIBE. — Here we have a relationship not 'by nature but by convention,'[1] 'by an appetency for the union,'[2] as Dicæarchus says. Notice the tribal

---

[1] 'Not φύσει but θέσει.'

[2] πόθῳ τῆς συνόδου. Partly owing to the misspelling, in Droysen's text, of one of them, these Greek words caused the translator much perplexity, for the dissipation of which he is not a little indebted to the accomplished Hellenist, Arnold Green, Esq., of Providence. They are from a fragment of Dicæarchus handed down by Stephanus of Byzantium, and are given by Carolus Mullerus, *Fragmenta Historicarum Græcarum*, vol. ii, p. 238, left hand column, § 9, as follows:

hero, the *gentilicia sacra*, racial and clan formations, *cognationes et propinquitates*, battles and cleavages.

§ 61.

(*d*) THE PEOPLE. — We have here to study commonwealths and religions as instituted by nature, the 'ethnic' age of the world, the fixedness and the mobility of peoples' types, in fact the whole subject of the so-called comparative psychology of peoples, and of 'Demology,' including the principle of nationality.

§ 62.

B. In the 'ideal partnerships' it is the task of the spiritual nature to find expression for itself and to pass over into the sphere of actual things, that thus it may be capable of being perceived and understood, becoming a bond between spirits, a common treasure.

§ 63.

(*a*) SPEECH AND THE LANGUAGES. — All thinking is speaking, moving in forms which language has evolved even when carrying these further. Vocal imitation is not mere mimicry of sound, but a translation of perceptions into vocal expression. Trace the successive stages of linguistic evolution, in multiplicity of forms, complexity of syntax, growth of specific

ὥστε πρότερον πόθῳ τῆς συνόδου γενομένης ἀδελφαῖς σὺν ἀδελφῷ ; or, as Müller prefers to read : ὥστε πόθῳ τῆς συνόδου τῆς πρότερον γενομένης. He is talking about the transference of a woman from one phratria to another, and says : "so that formerly, owing to the desire of coïtion of sisters with a brother, a different community of sacra was established." Müller prefers to make the *formerly* refer to the desire for coïtion rather than to the time of the establishment of the different community of sacred rites. — *Tr.*

meanings to words. Accordingly, by no means does 'the life of language cease where the life of History begins' (Schleicher). Study sound and writing, also the differences of thought-activity in languages, with phonetic writing and pictorial or ophthalmic languages.

§ 64.

(*b*) THE BEAUTIFUL AND THE ARTS. — Artistic imitation is no mere copying, mirroring, or echo, but the reproduction of an impression made upon the soul, sometimes even to the mistaking of one sense for another, as the *danseuse* dances the spring. Mark the ideal, and also the agreeableness of the imitation of it (Rumohr). The technical and the musical also fall here.

§ 65.

(*c*) THE TRUE AND THE SCIENCES. — Canvass scientific truth, the bearing of methods, the nature of skepticism, of doctrine, of hypothesis, of Nominalism and Realism.

§ 66.

(*d*) THE SACRED AND RELIGIONS. — Every religion is an expression of the need and helplessness of finite being, and of the need it has to know itself at the same time as enclosed in and with an infinite Being. It is an attempted expression of our feeling after God, of our confidence of sanctification and salvation through him, of our certainty of the Eternal, Perfect, and Absolute. Hence faith and worship, religion and theology, and the sacred history involved in every religion.

§ 67.

C. In the 'practical partnerships' move those interests which are contending and debatable, always at the same time bound together and driven on by men's natural needs, always called to and always pressing towards ideal ends or results, though never coming to any but a finitely perfect condition or a finitely satisfied rest.

§ 68.

(*a*) THE SPHERE OF SOCIETY. — Society assumes to offer to every man that position in which the moral partnerships shall best supplement him and he them. Here come up for review distinctions between classes, differences of blood and of culture, tradition and custom, the conservative elements of society, parties, public opinion, and so on; in fine, all that goes to constitute the social republic.

§ 69.

(*b*) THE SPHERE OF PROPERTY. — Economic organization assumes to embrace and to determine all the economic conditions and means necessarily pertaining to the moral partnerships : acquisition and competition, capital and labor, wealth and poverty, barter and money-exchange, the variation of values and the development of credit. Consider the State as a form of communism.

§ 70.

(*c*) THE SPHERE OF JUSTICE. — The system of justice assumes to give foundation to and to regulate all the jural forms in which the moral partnerships proceed.

Gauge here the reach of the sphere of justice. 'Justice must remain justice,' but also must wish to be nothing else. The modes of establishing it, putting it into operation and extending its scope are to be dwelt upon, as also the conception of the State as just an organ for securing justice (*Rechtsstaat*).

§ 71.

(*d*) THE SPHERE OF AUTHORITY. — The State assumes to be the sum, the united organism, of all the moral partnerships, their common home and harbor, and so far their end.

The State is the public power, offensive and defensive, both at home and abroad. In the life of the State and of States, authority is thus the essential thing, in the same way as love is in the sphere of the family, faith in the sphere of the church, the beautiful in the sphere of art, etc. The law of authority is valid in the political world like that of gravity in the world of matter. 'A ship a span long is no ship at all.'

Only the State has the duty or the right to be the authority in this sense. Wherever justice, property, society, wherever even the church, the people or the community come into the position of authority, the nature of the State is either not yet discovered or lost in degeneracy. Public authority is highest where the fullest labor, health and freedom of all the moral spheres feed it. The State is not related to the other moral spheres merely as they to one another, but embraces them all within its own scope. Under its protection and laws, under its guardianship and responsibility they all move forward to its salvation or ruin.

The State is not the sum of the individuals whom it comprehends, nor does it arise from their will, nor does it exist on account of their will.

The more rough the form of the State the more does force take in it the place of authority ; so much the poorer is it in freedom.

Out of the chaos of mere peoples State upon State crystallizes itself. Their relation to one another moves on from the *adversus hostem æterna auctoritas esto*,[1] to treaty and peaceful commerce and to international law. The Federal State, the confederation of States, the system of States, the world-system of States, — these are the ever further reaching wave-circles of this movement.

III THE WORK OF HISTORY IN RELATION TO THE WORKERS.

§ 72.

All changes and formations in the moral world are wrought by acts of will, as in the organic world everything is formed from cells. Acts of will are the efficients even where we say that the State, the people, the church, etc., do this and that.

§ 73.

Every human being is a moral subject ; only thus is he a human being. He has to build for himself his moral world (§ 47). In every individual, as a personality in part already developed and in part still the

---

[1] 'As against a foreigner your title shall be eternal.' Roman Law of the Twelve Tables.

subject of development, we feel an infinite interest. Witness how insatiably poetry and romance follow out and realize this interest.

Even the narrow, the very narrowest of human relations, strivings, activities, etc., have a process, a history, and are for the persons involved, historical. So family histories, local histories, special histories. But over all these and such histories is *History*.

§ 74.

As this marriage, this work of art, this State, stands related to the idea of the family, of the beautiful, of authority, so does the empirical, ephemeral 'I' (§ 55) stand related to that 'I' in which the philosopher thinks, the artist creates, the judge judges, the historian investigates. The Universal, this 'I' of humanity, is the subject of History. History is the γνῶθι σαυτὸν [1] of Humanity, its consciousness.

§ 75.

The life pulse of historical movement is freedom. The word 'freedom' has been understood differently at different times. Primarily it has only a negative meaning. The real meaning of freedom is unhindered participation in the life and work of each one of the moral spheres, not being disturbed or hampered in one of them by another, and not being excluded from any. Every one of them claims the whole of every man, not seldom to the total exclusion of the others. In the collision of duties, in the constantly painful perform-ance of these, and in the often crushing result, finite human nature sinks beneath the postulate of freedom.

[1] 'Know Thyself.'

§ 76.

The problem of the life of History is not to be sought in the false alternative between freedom and necessity. Necessity is the opposite of arbitrariness, accident, aimlessness; morality is the 'ought' — lying in the realm of the good, and is not subject to compulsion. Being free is the opposite of suffering compulsion, of being dead of will, destitute of 'I'; the moral is the willing of the good and is not subject to compulsion.

The highest freedom is to live for the highest good, for the end supreme (§ 46), toward which the movement of all movements, the science of which is History, is directed. Hence 'the full royal freedom of the moral man' (Fichte); hence the consecrating word, 'wherefore I do crown and mitre thee over thyself.' [1]

§ 77.

All movement in the historical world goes on in this way: Thought, which is the ideal counterpart of things as they really exist, develops itself as things ought to be; and characters, filled with the thought, bring the things to its standard. The condition of being thus filled with a thought is passion ($\pi\acute{a}\theta os$), which comes under obligation and responsibility in and through action, according to the old proverb, 'act much, suffer much.' [2]

§ 78.

Thoughts constitute the criticism of that which is and yet is not as it should be. Inasmuch as they may

[1] *Perch' io te sopra te corono e mitrio.* — Dante, *Purgatorio*, XXVII, 142. [2] δράσαντι παθεῖν. — Æschylus, *Choephori*, 313.

bring conditions to their level, then broaden out and harden themselves into accord with custom, conservatism and obstinacy, new criticism is demanded, and thus on and on.

The continuity of this censorship of thought, — 'those who hold the torch passing it from one to another'[1] — is what Hegel in his Philosophy of History calls 'the Dialectic of History.'

§ 79.

That out of the already given conditions new thoughts arise and out of the thoughts new conditions, — this is the work of men. The many, indeed, living only for their own interests and the business of the present, devoted to petty, ephemeral aims, following habit, the general stream, the nearest suggestions — these work for History without choice or will, in the bulk, unfreely. They are the noisy thyrsus-bearers in the festal train of the god, 'but few are the genuine Bacchanals' [βάκχοι δέ τε παῦροι].[2]

To anticipate the new thoughts in the movement of the moral world, to express them, to realize them, that is historical greatness, 'giving name to rolling time.'

IV. — THE WORK OF HISTORY IN RELATION TO ITS ENDS.

§ 80.

All development and growth is movement toward an end, which is to be fulfilled by the movement, thus

---

[1] λαμπάδα ἔχοντες διαδώσουσιν ἀλλήλοις.

[2] For the Greek, and the entire reference, see Plato, *Phaedo*, 69 C. —*Tr.*

coming to its realization. In the moral world end links itself to end in an infinite chain. Every one of these ends has primarily its own way to go and its own development to further, but at the same time each is a condition for the others and is conditioned by them. Often enough they repress, interrupt and contradict one another. Often appear here and there temporary and partial steps backwards; but always only that presently, with so much stronger advance and with exalted elasticity, work may be pushed forward at some new spot or in some new form, each form impelling the rest and impelled by them.

§ 81.

The highest end, which conditions without being conditioned, moving them all, embracing them all, explaining them all, that is, the supreme end (§ 15), is not to be discovered by empirical investigation.

Out of the self-consciousness of our 'I' (§ 12), out of the pressure of our moral will and our sense of obligation (§ 76), out of that longing after the one complete, eternal Being in whom our needy, ephemeral and fragmentary existence first feels its lack supplied, there reveals itself to us, in addition to the other 'proofs' of the existence of God, the one which is for us most demonstrative.

Evil cleaves to the finite spirit; it is the shadow of its finiteness when it is turned to the light. It belongs in the economy of the historical movement, but only 'as what vanishes in the process of things, destined for destruction.'

§ 82.

What their genus is to animals and plants — for the genus exists 'in order that they may participate in the timeless and the divine' [1] — that History is to human beings.

Ethics is the doctrine of the moral potencies and not merely that of the relations of persons to them and in them. Ethics and History are co-ordinates, as it were; for History furnishes the genesis of the 'postulate of the practical reason,' which postulate 'pure reason' could not discover.

§ 83.

History is humanity becoming and being conscious concerning itself. The epochs of History are not the life periods of this 'I' of Humanity — empirically we do not know whether this race 'I' is growing old or renewing its youth, only that it does not continue to be what it was or is, — but they are stages in that ego's self-knowledge, its knowledge of the world and of God.

§ 84.

According to the number of these traversed stages, grows the expression which man is able to form of the Supreme End, of his longing after it, and of the way to it. The fact that this expression broadens, enlarges and deepens itself with every stage, is the only thing which can wish to pass for the advancement of humanity.

§ 85.

To the finite eye beginning and end are veiled, but the direction of the streaming movement it can by in-

---

[1] ἵνα τοῦ ἀεὶ καὶ τοῦ θείου μετέχωσιν.

vestigation detect. Condemned to the narrow limit of
the here and the now, it yet dimly espies the whence
and the whither. It sees what it sees by being filled
with a light in which and from which everything is,
even its seeing being a remote reflection of that light
itself. The direct glory of that light our eye could
not bear, but practicing, clarifying, inflaming its vision
in the illuminated spheres which do disclose themselves
to it, it catches gleams of ever greater reaches, ever
more comprehensive empyreans. Among the circles
thus formed the human world with its history is one.
The historically great is only a mote in the sun-mist of
this manifestation of God.

§ 86.

History is Humanity's knowledge of itself, its certainty about itself. It is not 'the light and the truth,'
but a search therefor, a sermon thereupon, a consecra-
tion thereto. It is like John the Baptist, 'not that Light
but sent to bear witness of that Light.' [1]

THE DOCTRINE OF SYSTEMATIC
PRESENTATION.

§ 87.

As everything which moves the mind calls for a
corresponding expression wherein the mind may shape
it, so also the results of historical investigation need
their forms of expression — 'an exposition of history,'

[1] Οὐκ ἦν τὸ φῶς ἀλλ' ὅτι μαρτυρήσῃ περὶ τοῦ φωτός. — *John*, i : 8.

as Herodotus[1] has it — in order that the investigation may, as it were, give an account of what it has purposed and attained.

§ 88.

The forms of presentation here are not determined after the analogy of epic, lyric, or dramatic composition,[2] or by the 'distribution of time and space applied to the acts of human freedom in the State,'[3] or following the accidental medley of chronicles, remarkable events, pictures from antiquity, narratives 'of exploits in which the narrator personally took part ;'[4] but they are fixed by the double nature of the matter investigated.

The investigation which knows how, from the present and from certain elements given in the present and used by it as historical material, to produce ideas of processes and circumstances pertaining to past events, — such investigation has a double nature ; it is two things at once. It is the enrichment and deepening of the present by clearing up past events pertaining to it, and it is a clearing up of these past events by unlocking and unfolding certain remnants of them, remnants of facts which were relatively obscure and perhaps exceedingly so, even when present.

Still, in every case, however fruitful the investigation may have been, ideas arrived at by its aid are far from reaching the fullness of content, movement, manifoldness of forms and of real energy which the orginal things had when they constituted 'the present.' Always, moreover, whatever form may be chosen for the exposition of the results which investigation has brought

---

[1] ἱστορίης ἀπόδειξις.   [2] Gervinus.   [3] Wachsmuth.
[4] Aulus Gellius : *quibus rebus agendis interfuerit is qui narret.*

forth, this exposition will and can correspond only partially, in a certain way and from certain points of view, to the existence of things as they appeared when present, in the eyes of men then living and active. In this it is analogous to representations by graphic methods.

§ 89.

For a long time historical presentation satisfied itself with taking up views contained in oral and written sources, re-shaping them more or less, and recounting them afresh ; and the facts regarded through this illusion as 'transmitted,' passed for valid History, much as if the history of Alexander the Great's successors should pass as nothing but a succession of wars, because forsooth our sources for that period speak of scarcely anything else but wars. Only since we have begun to recognize Monuments and Remains as included in historical material and to avail ourselves of them methodically, has the investigation of past events gone deeper and planted itself on a firmer foundation. And with the discovery of the immeasurable gaps in our historical knowledge, which investigation has not yet filled up and perhaps now never can fill up, investigation espies ever wider breadths to the domains with which it has to do, and anticipates one day filling them with life. The presentation of the results of investigation will be more correct the more its consciousness of its ignorance equals that of its knowledge (§ 35).

§ 90.

(*a*) 'Interrogative exposition,' to set forth the result at which investigation has arrived, uses the form of investigation itself. This species of exposition is not a report or minute register of the actual investigation, including its false steps, errors and resultless measures, but it proceeds as if what has at last been discovered in the investigation were now first to be discovered or sought. It is a general imitation of preceding search or discovery. It may adopt the form of starting out from assumed ignorance with a question or a dilemma and seeking the true answer, as the advocate at the bar proceeds when he has to prove the so-called subjective fact from the objective; or the form of taking some certain datum, following up its signs and traces and finding further data at every step until at last the total result stands before us connected and complete. This course corresponds to that of the judge, who, in conducting an inquiry, has to infer the subjective fact from the objective. The former of these methods is the more convincing and demonstrative; the latter is the more dramatic and commands the attention better. For both it is essential to avoid what is so natural, introducing a chaos of irrelevant topics, casting less light upon the subject than upon the learned idleness of the author.

§ 91.

(*b*) 'Recitative exposition' sets forth the results of investigation as a course of events in imitation of its actual development. It takes those results and shapes from them an image of the genesis of the historical facts upon which investigation has been at work. It is only in appearance that the 'facts' in such a case speak for themselves, alone, exclusively, 'objectively.' Without the narrator to make them speak, they would

be dumb.   It is not objectivity that is the historian's
best glory.   His justness consists in seeking to understand.

Recitative exposition is possible in either of four forms:

(1) The 'pragmatic' shows how an event that was
premeditated or foreordained by fate, could occur, did
occur, and was forced to occur so and so, through the
movement of things converging upon that point.

(2) The 'monographic' shows how in its development and growth an historical formation grounded and
deepened itself and wrought itself out, brought forth
its genius, as it were.

(3) The 'biographical' shows how the genius of an
historical personality determined from the beginning
the action and suffering of that personality, and also
manifested and attested itself in the same.

(4) The 'catastrophic' shows various forms, tendencies, interests, parties, etc., each with some right on its
side, engaged in a battle, wherein the higher thought,
whose elements or sides display themselves in the
parties contending in the struggle, justifies and fulfils
itself by vanquishing and reconciling them.   This
species of exposition shows how out of the wars of the
Titans a new world and the new gods came into being.

§ 92.

(c) 'Didactic exposition' seizes the matter that has
been investigated, under the thought of its great historical continuity, in order to bring out its significance
as instruction for the present.   History is not instructive
in consequence of affording patterns for imitation or
rules for new application, but through the fact that we

mentally live it over again and live according to it. 'It is a repertory of ideas furnishing matter which judgment must needs put into the crucible in order to purify it.'[1]

Finished intellectual training is culture. This is military, legal, theological, if intended for these callings, or general culture if it has the aim of exercising and developing in us not this or that individual or technical ability, but the human qualities in general. It may then be well termed 'Humanity,' for 'precisely the course whereby the human race arrived at its perfection, every individual human being must have passed over' (Lessing).

In the conception of this author's 'Education of the Human Race,' culture — apart from special and technical — derives its matter as well as its forms (§ 6) from History. And indeed the fact that the great movements of History complete themselves in a small circle of typical formations, the greatest in a still smaller circle, makes it possible valuably to apply History in a didactic way not only to the higher and even the highest needs, but also to the elementary.

Are there forms of historical presentation for this purpose? Are Herder's presentations of Universal History, or Schlözer's, Johannes von Müller's, Leo's, or von Ranke's, patterns for this kind of historical composition?

No one will measure the worth of the sermon in the Evangelical Church by printed sermons, still less desire

---

[1] Frederic the Great, *Œuvres*, IV, p. xvii : *C'est un répertoire d'idées qui fournit de la matière que le jugement doit passer au creuset pour l'épurer.*

the enforcement of a canon securing for every Sunday a sermon according to a prescribed pattern. Rather should every sermon be a new witness to the living evangelical spirit in our Church ; and so far as the congregation is edified by them they are so.

The correct form of didactic exposition is the historical instruction of youth. Particularly is this so where it is in the hands of a teacher who moves in the fields of History as master, with the highest possible freedom and independence as an investigator, and by communicating his instruction in ever new shapes and turns bears witness to the spirit that fills and bears on the life of History.

§ 93.

(*d*) 'Discussive exposition' takes the total result of the investigation, gathers all its rays as in a concave mirror, and turns them upon some definite point of present interest, throwing light upon it thus in order to 'set it clear.' It may be some question to be decided, some pair of alternatives which is to yield a choice, or some new phenomenon the understanding of which is to be mastered. To everything new, not only political facts, but also fresh discoveries, recent efforts in art and science, etc., historical elucidation and comparison has to assign its place in the progressive course and sweep of human endeavor. We here refer to criticism, scientific, æsthetic, of the publicist, etc.

The points to be established in any given discussion lie partly within the subject discussed, as that this nation, this power, this church, etc., has had, in virtue of its historical antecedents, such or such a character. For instance, the old '*sint ut sunt aut non sint*'. But

also in outside matters simply conditioning and determining the subject, and in fact in the whole congeries
of events prevailing at any moment, the elements which
give broad determination to its historical connection
are to be found, interpreted and applied.

The essence of theory is that it gathers from the
shaping and elaborating process of investigation its net
results, and imparts to them the form of a principle, a
lawgiving conclusion, with, indeed, a legitimate claim
to this character. The more the theory has failed to
sum up all the elements, the more one-sidedly it brings
into prominence what lies nearest or is least active,
the more doctrinaire it is. This appears in that the
determinative element, which at any given time led to
the further step, was, with its favoring nature, present
and operative only for that case, under those circumstances, for that end.

Every State has its own politics, domestic as well as
foreign. Discussion, even in the press, in the council
of state, and in parliament, is reliable in proportion as
it is historical ; ruinous in the degree in which it bases
itself upon mere doctrines, or upon idols of the theater,
forum, den and tribe.

The practical significance of historical studies lies in
the fact that they, and they alone, hold up before the
State, or people, or army, its own picture. Especially is
historical study the basis for political improvement and
culture. The statesman is the historian in practice,
'able to see into realities, and to do the things that are
to be done.'[1] The State is, however, but the most
complex among the organisms belonging to the moral

---

[1] Θεωρητικὸς τῶν ὄντων καὶ πρακτικὸς τῶν δεόντων.

potencies. Every formation of the kind requires similar self-control through discussion. We may specify ecclesiastical government, the conduct of industrial undertakings, the arrangement of a scientific expedition, and such things.

§ 94.

With the last named form of exposition our science indeed enters wide realms; but it cannot forbear to affirm its authority also in these, in the same way as the natural sciences have no hesitation in proceeding to demonstrate their value wherever their methods show themselves applicable. Even the investigations and results of the natural sciences are not the work of abstract observation and experiment, as if they uttered no voice save that of the facts which have been observed and interrogated. It is the mighty total of repeated yet enlarging life-experiences displaying itself in the continuity of History; it is this which first gives to the minds investigating in this field the elevation and compass of views and thoughts enabling them thus to observe and get things ready to be questioned, thus to combine and conclude. The same is true of the speculative sciences. For all growth in men's thinking and invention, in their creative activity, determination and efficiency, proceeds in respect to forms exclusively, and to a great extent in respect to materials, from these laboriously gotten results and repeated life experiences, to investigate whose continuity is the task of History.

§ 95.

Our science does not pretend that its method of investigation is the only scientific one (§ 14). It con-

tents itself with being able in its expositions of results,
to give only so much as its province and investigation
enable it to get, only so much as its methods put within
its powers.   And the more questions there are in its
various departments which it is conscious of being no
longer or not yet able satisfactorily to answer, the more
careful it will be about pretending that its result is
greater than it legitimately is or can be.   The aim of
the historical expositor thus is to afford an idea elaborated in the most certain measure possible and developed
in the closest possible accord with facts, of things which
were present and actual, whether in recent, distant or
most ancient times, though they now live and have a
contemporary character only in the knowledge of men.

APPENDICES.

I. — The Elevation of History to the Rank of a Science.

BEING A REVIEW OF THE HISTORY OF CIVILIZATION IN ENGLAND,[1] BY H. T. BUCKLE.

OUR age is fond of boasting that no preceding one equals it in the freedom and boldness with which it works or in the magnitude or the practical character of its results. True, and we must, without envy, give the prize to the natural sciences for what they accomplish toward this result, and for the way in which they accomplish it.

The energy of these branches of learning comes from their having a completely clear consciousness of their problems, their means, their methods, and from the fact that they consider the things which they draw into the compass of their investigations under those points of view, and those only, upon which their method is based.

A French investigator strikingly characterizes this field of studies in the following often cited words : ' Whenever we can transfer one of the vital phenomena to the class of the physical, we have made a new conquest in the sciences, whose realm is thereby so much enlarged. In such a case, facts take the place of words, analysis of hypothesis ; the laws of organic bodies fall together with those of inorganic, and like them become susceptible of explanation and simplification.'

[1] Vol. I, ed. 2, London, 1858.   Vol. II, 1861.

But this judgment here appears in a universal form, whose legitimacy is more than questionable. Is it, indeed, true that a new conquest is made in science only when vital phenomena are transferred to the class of physical? Would that be, in fact, a correct definition of the essence and scope of science? Should the other realms of human discovery be obliged to recognize themselves as of a scientific nature only in so far as they are in a condition to transfer vital phenomena to the class of physical phenomena?

It is not alone the astonishing performance and results of work in natural science which spreads abroad the conviction that its method is in a preëminent measure scientific, the only scientific one. The deeper ground of popularity attaching to that way of looking at things whose counterpart is in the world of quantitative phenomena, lies in the mode of culture prevalent in our age, and in that stage of development at which we have arrived socially and politically.

Buckle is not the first who has attempted to treat the unscientific character of History, the ' methodless matter,' [1] as an ancient writer names it, by the method of exhibiting vital phenomena under points of view analogous to those which are the starting-point of the exact sciences. But a notion which others have incidentally broached under some formula about ' natural growth,' or carried out in the very inadequate and merely figurative idea of the inorganic ; what still others, as Comte in his attractive *'Philosophie Positive,'* have developed speculatively, Buckle undertakes to ground in a comprehensive historical exposition.

[1] ἀμέθοδος ὕλη.   See page 107.

He speaks with sharp expressions of the 'guild of historians' and their doings hitherto, of the poverty of thought under which they have labored, and the absence of principles in their investigations. He thinks that, working in their way, 'every bootmaker is fitted for a writer of history.' 'If, through indolence of thought or natural limitation he is not capable of handling the highest branches of knowledge, he needs only to apply a few years to the reading of a certain number of books, and he may write the history of a great people and attain consideration in his profession.' Mr. Buckle finds that 'as regards all higher tendencies of human thinking, History still lies in deplorable incompleteness and presents so confused and anarchical an appearance as were to be expected only in case of a subject with unknown laws or destitute as yet even of a foundation.'

He purposes to raise History to a science by showing how to demonstrate historical facts out of general laws. He paves the way for this by setting forth that the earliest and rudest conceptions touching the course of human destiny were those indicated by the ideas of chance and necessity, that 'in all probability' out of these grew later the 'dogmas' of free will and predestination, that both are in great degree 'mistakes,' or that, as he adds, 'we at least have no adequate proof of their truth.' He finds that all the changes of which History is full, all the vicissitudes which have come upon the human race, its advance and its decline, its happiness and its misery, must be the fruit of a double agency, the working of outer phenomena upon our nature and the working of our nature upon outer phenomena.' He has confidence that he has discovered the 'laws' of this double influence, and that he has therefore elevated the History of mankind to a science.

Buckle sees the peculiar historical content of Humanity's life in that which he calls Civilization. He has traced the history of civilization among the English, French, Spanish, and Scotch, that he may illustrate by these examples the application of his method and the justification of the laws discovered by him. He arrives at these laws, as he says, in the two only possible ways, deduction and induction. He proceeds deductively in showing how the historical development of civilization is explained by these laws, and inductively in that he gathers out of the multitudinous facts which he has collected in his studies the standard and important ones, and finds the higher expression that unites them.

I will not attempt to criticise his induction and deduction from the point of view of the historical material brought forward in substantiation of them. There might be in his manner of employing sources, in the choice of his statements, in the fitness of his combinations, a large and constant intermixture of error, caprice and inadequacy — as is actually the case — without lessening the scientific importance of the problem which he introduces to our science or of the method which he recommends for its solution. Buckle the historian would only have retired behind Buckle the philosopher, and it would remain for professional historians to exemplify and test the great discovery presented by him better than the gifted dilettant in our studies could do.

Von Sybel's *Zeitschrift* contained some time ago a few instructive essays upon Historical Method and the mode and reach of historical knowledge, showing also how guardedly History should deal with those questions which, never of a purely historical nature, must yet be treated and in her way solved by our science, unless she is willing to run the risk of having problems offered her, paths prescribed for her and definitions of science thrust upon her from a foreign source, to which she cannot agree without self-renunciation, without giving over that calling in the field of human knowledge which she and she alone can fulfil.

The recognition will not be denied to historical studies that even they have some part in the intellectual movement of our age, that they are active in discovering the new, in investigating anew what has been transmitted, and in presenting results in appropriate forms. But when asked their scientific justification and their relation to the other circles of human knowledge, when asked what is the foundation of their procedure, what the connection of their means and their problems, they are up to date in no condition to give satisfactory information. However earnestly and thoroughly individual members of our 'guild' may have thought through these questions, our science has not yet set its theory and system on a firm footing. Meantime we console ourselves with the thought that it is not only a science but also an art, and perhaps — at least according to the judgment of the public — an art more than a science.

We in Germany have slight ground to ignore the high importance of advanced technique in our studies, of our increasing practice and certitude in historical criticism, or of the results which have been reached through these means. The quest which concerns us

here is another. A work like Buckle's is well adapted
to remind us how very unclear, contradictory and beset
with arbitrary opinions the foundations of our science
are. And the deep impression which the work has
made not only upon the numerous lovers of each newest
paradox, be it table-rapping, phalanstery, or the olive
leaf of the friends of peace, but also on many younger
adherents of historical studies, may well be a warning
to us at last to seek after the foundation of our science
too, in certitude about which the natural sciences since
Bacon — unless he is for other reasons undeserving of
place at the head of the development — are in advance
of us.

Now is it Buckle's merit to have achieved his purpose? Can he have developed the true meaning and
idea of the historical branches of learning or fixed the
extent of their application? Is he the Bacon of the
historical sciences and his work the Organon to teach
us to think historically? Has the method which he
propounds power to remove from the realms of historical knowledge the idols of the den, forum, theatre, and
so on, which even to-day obscure our sight in the form
of the 'errors', as he calls them, of free-will and divine
providence, the over-valuation of the moral principle in
relation to the intellectual, and the like? And if he is
really right in appealing for the most interesting of his
fundamental propositions, that touching free-will, to our
Kant, who, like Buckle himself, as Buckle thinks,
regarded 'the reality of free-will in the world of phenomena as an untenable assumption,' can he claim pri-
ority in the discovery just made in Germany with such
lively acclaim, that Kant's teaching is precisely the re-

verse of what has hitherto been supposed, and that the result of Kant's two Critiques is that both are false?

Buckle's translator adverts to the fact that up to the present time the Kantian philosophy has been the extreme limit to which English thinkers have ventured. He calls Buckle's philosophy 'incomplete thinking, in which crude criticism passes as philosophy,' and charges upon his author, in spite of the Vedas and of Cousin and Kant, the only non-English authorities he quotes, 'a truly antique consciousness touching all proper thought.' When, however, he greets the laws found by Buckle 'as a splendid and entirely truthful program of the progress of the human mind,' and speaks of the reformer's *rôle* which the work is to play even in Germany, the utterances badly embarrass us. Must we, an 'antistrophe' as it were to our former statement, admit that a large element of error, inadequacy and antiqueness runs right through Buckle's philosophical buttressing of his theory, yet does not lessen the reformatory significance of his work, this being injured as little by the philosophical as by the historical dilettantism of the author?

Perhaps, free from the scholastic 'anticipations' of both these two departments, and so able to canvass the more impartially the question of the nature and laws of History, Buckle can point out the way, so clear to every sound human understanding, by which History is to be raised to the rank of a science. He repeatedly confesses that he wishes to observe and argue entirely and only as an empiricist. At least the great and simple outlines of the empirical procedure, provided vision is not obscured by prepossessions, appear plain to the so-called sound human understanding without explanation. Such an understanding is precisely what the English mean when they dub 'philosophical' those natural sciences whose laurels do not permit our investigators to rest. Buckle hopes, he says, 'to accomplish for the History of mankind that or something similar to that which other investigators have achieved in the natural sciences, where occurrences apparently the most irregular and contradictory have been explained and proved to accord with certain unchangeable and general laws. If we subject the processes of the human world to a similar treatment, we certainly have every prospect of a similar result.'

It is of interest to notice the *quid pro quo* from which Buckle starts out. Can any one 'who believes in the possibility of a science of History,' as he himself does and as he is certain that by applying the method of natural science he has established the propriety of doing, fail to notice that this method does not so much raise History to a science by itself as it places it among the natural sciences? Other sciences, too, such as theology and philosophy, at the times when their methods passed for the only scientific ones, believed that they were entitled to take History and nature under their jurisdiction, but neither the knowledge of Nature nor that of History was thereby advanced in the measure intended by those interested in orthodoxy or speculation. Is there, then, never more than one way, one method of knowledge? Do not its methods incessantly vary according to their objects, like the organs of sense with the different forms of sensuous perception, and like organs in general with their diverse functions?

Whoever believes in the possibility of a science of History,' thinking logically and according to the nature of the matter in hand, as we do in Germany, would certainly never undertake to show us the justness of this belief by pretending that one can smell with the hands as well as touch, digest with the feet, see tones and hear colors. To be sure, the vibrations of a string which the ear perceives as a deep tone can also be seen by the eye ; but the property of these vibrations enabling them to be perceived as tone does not exist for the eye. It is a fact solely for the ear and for its peculiar method of perception. It is true that in the departments with which the ' science of History ' has to do, there is much which is level and accessible to natural-scientific method also, as well as to various other forms of scientific knowledge. But since phenomena, however many or few, since points of view and relations remain which are accessible to none of the other kinds of knowledge, it is clear that there must be for them another method, special and particular. If there is to be a ' science of History,' in which we too believe, this means that there exists a circle of phenomena for which neither the theological, the philosophical, the mathematical nor the physical manner of consideration is adapted, that there are questions to which speculation gives no answer, whether, theologically, it have the absolute for its point of departure, or, philosophically, take it for its goal ; which are equally unanswered by that empiricism which apprehends the world of phenomena by its quantitative procedure, and by any discipline pertaining to the practical departments of the moral world.

Our founder of the science of History approaches his task with enviable *naïveté*. He considers it unnecessary to investigate the ideas with which he intends to work, or to limit off the department in which his laws find their application. What science is he thinks every one knows, and the same of History. Not quite, after all, for he takes particular pains to state what it is not. He cites with hearty assent Comte, *Philosophie Positive*, V. p. 18, who remarks with displeasure that 'it is entirely inappropriate to characterize as History the piling up of disconnected facts.' How memorable is this sentence of the French thinker, and how instructive it is that the Englishman appropriates it to himself! We of course designate as 'History' that infinite succession of objective facts in which we see the life of men, of nations, of humanity going on, just as we embrace the totality of another kind of phenomena under the name of 'Nature.' But pray has anyone ever thought that a collection of dried plants constituted Botany, or a lot of stuffed or unstuffed animal skins Zoölogy? Did anyone ever suppose it even possible to collect and pile together, whether in an orderly or in a disorderly way, purely objective facts, such as battles, revolutions, business crises, foundings of cities, and the like? Has 'the guild of historians' actually not yet made the observation that objective facts are a different thing from the manner in which we know them?

If Buckle really wished to kindle a light for us historians groping in the dark, he should first of all have made it clear to himself and to us how and with what right 'History' has been able to fix itself as name for a definite series of phenomena, as 'Nature' has suc-

ceeded in making itself the name of another definite
series of manifestations. He should have shown what
it means that the wonderful abridger, the human spirit,
apprehends spatial manifestations as Nature and temporal occurrences as History ; not because they are so and
so distinguished objectively, but in order to be able to
grasp and think them. He would then have known
the nature of the material with which a 'science of
History' can have to do. If he had been aware what
it means to have been an empiricist, he would not have
omitted to investigate, as the nature of all empiricism
demands, the manner in which these materials of historical investigation lie before us and our sense-perception
at the present time. Then surely he would have had
to recognize that not past events, not the infinite confusion of 'facts' which constituted them, now lie before us
as materials for investigation ; that instead these facts
vanished forever with the moment to which they belonged, and that, as human, we possess only the present,
the here and now, with the impulse and ability, of
course, by learning, insight, and will, to develop immeasurably this ephemeral point. He would have seen
that among the processes peculiar to the realm of the
spirit, one of the most remarkable is that which makes
it possible for us again to awaken to present reality
events which are forever past and now lie behind us,
and to make them live in our minds, that is, to all
human intents and purposes, make them eternal.

If Buckle had wished to raise us and himself above
his thoughtless use of the word 'History,' with the
anticipations which arise out of this and dim our vision,
he would have had to take us on into a second line of

considerations. In occasional intimations of his we
ascertain that History has to do with the 'actions of
men,' that it is connected 'with the unsatisfied desire
for knowledge which characterizes our fellowmen';
but he omits to tell us in what manner these actions of
men are of an historical nature, and leaves us in the
dark touching the character of the questions for which
the curiosity displayed by our fellowmen seeks answer.

It does not require deep penetration to see that the
human acts which are now historical, at the moment
when they happened and in the minds of those through
whom and for whom they happened, had only in the
rarest instances the purpose or determination to be
historical deeds. The general who gives battle, the
statesman who negotiates a treaty, has quite enough to
do to attain the practical end which concerns him at
the moment. So on down to the minute and even the
minutest 'acts of men': they all fulfil themselves in
that illimitably manifold interplay of interests, conflicts,
businesses, of motives, passions, forces and restrictions,
the sum of which has been well named the moral world.
We may consider these under very various points of
view, practical, technical, legal, social, etc. One of the
ways in which the moral world may be surveyed is
the historical.

I decline to set forth the full bearing of these
observations. The attentive reader will see that, were
this done, it would become clear how History (*Geschichte*) emerges, so to speak, out of men's doings
(*Geschäften*). We should also thus learn of what
sort and nature that knowledge is which is based
on such materials and applicable in such a realm;

what it can and cannot do; what kind of certainty
it is in condition to give, and what kind of truth it
is calculated to ascertain.

Buckle has the goodness to recognize that belief in
the value of History is widely extended, and that historical material has been collected which on the whole
enjoys and commands profound attention and respect.
He depicts in broad outlines what a mass of investigations and discoveries has been already made in the field
of History.   But, he adds, 'if we were to tell how
little this material has been utilized, we should have to
sketch quite another picture.'   How little it has been
utilized !   Must everything therein be explored before
any body of facts is a science ?   Is the astonishing
depth of mathematical knowledge scientific only because
the surveyor or the mechanician can use one or two
propositions from it ?   When the prophets, to warn and
punish the Israelites, held before them the image of
themselves, how different was the result from what
followed when they pointed out how the God of their
fathers had testified to them 'all the way from Egypt.'
When Thucydides wrote his History with its 'perpetual
value' ($\kappa\tau\hat{\eta}\mu\alpha$ $\epsilon\hat{\iota}s$ $\dot{\alpha}\epsilon\acute{\iota}$), ought he to have meant by this
proud phrase the artistic form in which he wrote and
not the historical drama of which he wrote ?   Buckle's
reproachful question forgets that the work of the
centuries is the entail of each new generation.   In
what else does the civilization so highly extolled by
himself consist but in the summed up work of those
who were before us ?   All past events, the whole of
'History,' is ideally contained in the present and in
that which the present possesses.   And when we bring

to our consciousness this ideal content of History ; when
we represent to ourselves in a kind of narrative form
how that which is has come to pass, what else do we
thus do but employ History in understanding that which
is, the elements in which we move as thinking, volitional
and active beings ? This is the way, or at least one of
the ways, immeasurably to extend, enrich and elevate
the needy and lonesome Here and Now of our ephemeral
existence. In proportion as we, — I mean the working
races of men — ascend higher, the horizon which we
survey is extended, and with every new point of view
each particular element thereof displays itself to us in
new perspectives, in new and wider relations. The
width of our horizon is almost exactly the measure of
the height reached by us ; and in the same measure has
the circle of the resources, conditions, and tasks of our
existence extended. History gives us the consciousness
of what we are and have.

Here is a connection of thought, it is worth while
to notice, whence one may see what culture is and
what it means to us. Goethe says : ' What thou
hast inherited from thy ancestors, earn in order to
possess it.' We find here the justification of this
obscure utterance. However high may be the position
of the age or of the nation into which we individuals
are born, however great or full the inheritance accruing
to our advantage without our coöperation, so long as
we have not gained it through our own efforts and have
not recognized it as that which it is, the result of in-
cessant toil on the part of those who were before us,
we hold it as if we had it not. Now culture means
that we have lived and toiled through over again, as a

continuation, that which has, in the History of times, peoples and humanity, been wrought out in men's spirit in the way of thought. Civilization is satisfied only with the results of culture. Amid utmost fullness of mere wealth, it is poor, *blasé* with opulence of enjoyment.

After Buckle has complained how little the rich and ever-growing 'mass of facts' has hitherto been utilized, he assigns as a reason explaining this phenomenon a 'peculiarly unfortunate circumstance.' 'In all the other great departments of investigation,' he says, 'the necessity of generalization is admitted by every one, and we meet with noble exertions, based on specific facts, to reveal the laws under whose rule the facts stand. Historians on the contrary are so far from making this procedure their own as to be dominated by the strange thought that their business is solely to recount transactions, enlivening these at the utmost with appropriate moral and political remarks.'

A certain patience is necessary to follow these repetitious trivialities and this confusion of ideas which chase each other around in a circle. Generalizations then are the laws which Buckle seeks. He thinks it possible in the way of generalization to find the laws which shall reveal, that is, determine with necessity, the phenomena of the moral world. Then are the rules of a language linguistic laws? To be sure, induction sums up particulars into the general fact ; not, however, simply by arriving at a generality hap-hazard, but by combining particulars in that which is really common to them. But to proceed from the rule to the law, to find the ground for the general phenomenon, there is need of analytical procedure. Buckle does not consider it necessary to give himself and us any account of the logic of his investigation. He satisfies himself with setting aside a 'preliminary hindrance' which seems to block his way. 'It is supposed,' says he, 'that there is in human things something providential and mysterious, which makes them impervious to our investigation and will conceal from us forever their future course.' He meets this difficulty with the 'simple' alternative: 'Are the acts of men and hence also of society subject to definite laws, or are they the result either of accident or of supernatural influence?' Certainly: if this cloud is not a camel, it is either a weasel or a whale.

We have already remarked that if there is to be a science of History, this must have its own method of discovery and relate to its own department of knowledge. If in other fields induction or deduction has rendered excellent results, it does not follow that the science of History must employ exclusively the one or the other of those methods. Fortunately there are between heaven and earth things related as irrationally to deduction as to induction; which demand deduction and synthesis along with induction and analytical treatment; which are grasped by being subjected alternately to both procedures; which even then are not entirely comprehended, but more and more, not exhaustively but approximately and in a certain way; things which demand not to be 'developed' or 'explained' but understood.

The 'desire for knowledge which characterizes our fellow men' is 'insatiable' because whatever it brings to us is rationally comprehensible, and because with our growing understanding of man and of what exists and

develops in a human fashion, that which is most truly
our own becomes wider, deeper, freer, indeed only then
becomes ours. Certain as it is that we human beings
also weave our lives into the general mutation of matter,
and correct as it may be that every individual temporarily comprises and has for his form of existence only
just such and such atoms out of 'eternal matter,'
equally and in fact infinitely more certain is it that by
means of these 'fleeting formations' and their forces,
so vital after all, something quite unique and incompar-
able has sprung up and is still springing up, a second
creation, not of new materials but of forms, of thoughts,
of societies with their virtues and duties, in a word, the
Moral World.

In this realm of the moral world everything is accessible to our understanding, from the most insignificant
love-story to great state transactions, from the solitary
mental work of the poet or the thinker to the immeasurable combinations of the world's commerce, or
poverty's struggle so beset with temptation. Whatever exists we may understand, inasmuch as we can
apprehend it as something that has developed from
beginnings.

It has already been mentioned that Buckle does not
so much leave the freedom of the will, in connection
with divine providence, out of view, but rather declares
it an illusion and throws it overboard. Within the pre-
cincts of philosophy also something similar has recently
been taught. A thinker whom I regard with personal
esteem says : 'If we call all that an individual man is,
has and performs A, then this A arises out of $a + x$,
a embracing all that comes to the man from his outer

circumstances : from his country, people, age, etc., while the vanishingly little x is his own contribution, the work of his free will.' However vanishingly small this x may be, it is of infinite value. Morally and humanly considered it alone has value. The colors, the brush, the canvas which Raphael used were of materials which he had not created. He had learned from one and another master to apply these materials in drawing and painting. The idea of the Holy Virgin and of the saints and angels, he met with in church tradition. Various cloisters ordered pictures from him at given prices. That this incitement alone, these material and technical conditions and such traditions and contemplations, should 'explain' the Sistine Madonna, would be, in the formula $A = a + x$, the service of the vanishingly little x. Similarly everywhere. Let statistics go on showing that in a certain country so and so many illegitimate births occur. Suppose that in the formula $A = a + x$ this a includes all the elements which 'explain' the fact that among a thousand mothers twenty, thirty, or whatever the number is, are unmarried; each individual case of the kind has its history, how often a touching and affecting one. Of those twenty or thirty who have fallen is there a single one who will be consoled by knowing that the statistical law 'explains' her case? Amid the tortures of conscience through nights of weeping, many a one of them will be profoundly convinced that in the formula $A = a + x$ the vanishingly little x is of immeasurable weight, that in fact it embraces the entire moral worth of the human being, his total and exclusive value.

No intelligent man will think of denying that the statistical method of considering human affairs has its great worth; but we must not forget how little, relatively, it can accomplish and is meant to accomplish. Many and perhaps all human relations have a legal side; yet no one will on that account bid us seek for the understanding of the Eroica [1] or of Faust among jurists' definitions concerning intellectual property.

I will not follow Buckle in his further discussions touching the 'laws of nature,' 'mental laws,' the superiority of the intellectual over the moral forces, and so on. The essence of his views in the first part he sums up at the beginning of the second, in the following four 'generic thoughts,' which pass according to him for the foundations of a History of Civilization. '1. The progress of the human race depends upon the effect with which the laws of phenomena are investigated and the extent to which the results of these investigations are made known. 2. Before such an investigation can begin, a spirit of scepticism must be awakened, which then in turn furthers investigation and is furthered by it. 3. The discoveries made in this manner strengthen the influence of intellectual truths and weaken relatively, though not absolutely, the influence of moral truths, the latter being in consequence less subject to growth and development than the intellectual truths. 4. The chief enemy of this movement and hence the chief enemy of civilization is the paternal or guardianship spirit, the idea, namely, that human society can not prosper unless its affairs

[1] The *Sinfonia Eroica*, of Beethoven. See Grove, *Beethoven's Nine Symphonies.* — *Tr.*

are watched over and protected at every step by State and Church, the State teaching men what to do, the Church what to believe.'

If these are the laws in which 'the study of the History of humanity' is to attain scientific elevation, then the happy discoverer is truly an object of envy in the *naïveté* with which he succeeds in deceiving himself even for a single moment as to their extraordinary shallowness. Laws of this sort could be discovered daily by the dozen, in the self-same way of generalization, laws none of which would in depth and fruitfulness be inferior to the well known saying that the measure of a people's civilization is its consumption of soap.

Bacon somewhere says that 'truth emerges more readily from error than from confusion.'[1] The confusion of which Buckle is guilty is obvious. Because he neglected to examine and sound the nature of the subjects with which he undertook to deal, he proceeds with them as if they did not have any nature or character of their own at all and so did not need a method of their own; and the method which he does apply in this department so foreign to it, avenges itself by making him put up with commonplaces instead of the calculable formulas in which it elsewhere expresses its laws : commonplaces which may have a certain propriety for to-day and yesterday, but which, in face of History's milleniums, in face of the great social formations of the middle age, of beginning Christianity, and of the Greek and Roman world, appear entirely unmeaning.

[1] *Citius emergit veritas ex errore quam ex confusione.*

If Buckle recognizes the great work of the human race in History, how could he help asking himself the nature of this work, out of what material and for what ends it has originated, and how the workers are related to it? Had he done this he would — for it is worth while to pause a moment over these questions — have recognized that historical work embraces, in respect to its material, both natural data and historical growths, and that each constitutes for it at once a means and a limitation, at once condition and impulse. He would have noticed that in this department the method of quantitative phenomena has of course a certain applicability, and that where we have to do with the great factors of bodily existence, of natural conditions, of statistical results, our branch of learning will accompany the labors of exact science with the greatest interest and accept its splendid products with pleasure and gratitude. But if Buckle had been mindful of the further questions referred to, he would have saved himself from thinking that the conclusions arrived at in that department — the laws ascertained, as he thinks, in the way of generalization — are the sum of History and 'raise History to the rank of a science' by 'explaining' its phenomena. This explains them as little as the beautiful statue of The Praying Boy [1] is explained by the bronze out of which it was poured, the clay which formed the model of it, or the fire which melted the metal. The idea of the image that was to be (τὸ τί ἦν εἶναι) was necessary, as 'the master of those who know' long ago taught, and this was in the

[1] In the Old Museum, Berlin. It is believed to be from an original of the time of Lysippus. Frederic the Great purchased it for 10,000 Thaler [$7,500]. — Tr.

artist's soul before the work in which it was to be
realized existed. There was need also of the purpose
which the statue should fulfil, perhaps a vow to the
rescuing god whose temple it was to adorn. The skilful
hand, too, was required, to put together the motive,
the thought-image and the material into the completed
work. Doubtless the bronze as well was necessary in
order to the origination of The Praying Boy ; yet it
would take a mean civilization to appraise this wonderful work of art only at the value of the metal in it, as
Buckle does with History.

Buckle proceeds not a whit less one-sidedly than
those people — how severely he censures them ! — who
explain History solely from the motive which theology,
for instance, ascribes to it, or the religious spirit sur-
mises as dominant in it ; or those who see and observe
in respect to any work only the deft [*geschickt*] agents
which perform it, just as if the fates [*Geschicke*] did
not take their course in spite of the good or evil will
of the people through whom they are put in execution ;[1]
or those who, always on hand with their ready-made
static ideas and doctrines about things which are continually developing and thus criticising themselves,
always just know and know better than any one else
how the State, the Church, the social order, etc., ought
to have been obliged to exist and develop. Each of
these ways of viewing things is in itself partial, untrue,
destructive, even though each is in a sense justified
and necessary. 'Everything,' teaches the ancient
philosopher just referred to, 'everything which subsists

[1] The author intended a play upon the two words in the brackets,
but in using them confuses rather than clarifies his meaning. — *Tr.*

by the agency of a cause, and is not, like the divinity, self-subsistent,' contains those four elements,[1] no one of which alone and by itself can explain the whole. More precisely, it is according to those four elements that we mentally analyze anything for ourselves, for our contemplation, conscious that in the reality which we wish to consider they are at the same time completely one with and permeated by each other. We thus separate and distinguish, although aware that the process is only an aid to our re-constructive understanding, while certain other activities of our soul give and receive totalities instantly and immediately.

Pardon these very elementary observations. In view of Buckle's confused procedure they could not have been avoided if the questions involved were to be gotten onto a safer track.

We see that in History the material upon which it works is not the only thing to be considered. Close to the material comes the form. In its varying forms History has a ceaseless and ever progressive life. These forms are the moral partnerships in which we become bodily and spiritually what we are, and by virtue of which we raise ourselves above the miserable desolation and indigence of our atomic egoism, giving and receiving in order thus to become the richer the more we bind and obligate ourselves. These are departments in which laws of an entirely different nature and energy from those which the new science seeks, have their place and exercise their power. These moral forces,

---

[1] Referred to on pages 81, 82, viz., the material, the form, the moving cause, and the end or final cause. The thought is from Aristotle. — *Tr.*

as they have been finely termed, are to a great degree at once factors and products of the historical life. Ceaselessly developing, they, by what they have at any time come to be, determine who shall be thereafter the bearers of their completed products, and raise them above themselves. In the community of the family, the State, the nation, etc., the individual has lifted himself above the narrow boundary of his ephemeral ego, in order, if I may so speak, to think and act as prompted by the ego of the family, the nation, and the State. In this elevation and undisturbed participation in the activity of the moral forces, according to each man's character and duty, not in the unlimited and boundless independence of the individual, lies the true essence of freedom. Without the moral forces it is nothing ; it is immoral, a mere power of movement.

Of these moral forces Buckle certainly holds a very low opinion. In Church and State he sees nothing but guardianship and encroachments. To him right and law are only barriers and impediments. The consequence of his manner of view would be not so much to refer the child to the care and love of its parents and the discipline and guidance of its teachers, as rather to consider it by and for itself a manifestation of sovereign liberty.

Buckle arrives at such an extraordinarily crude idea of liberty because he neglects proper attention to the agents engaged in working out History's task ; because he thinks only of the massed capital known as civilization, not of the ever new acquisition which forms the essence of culture. Moreover, he does not or will not

see that in that vanishingly little x lies the whole and
the only worth of personality, a worth which is not
measured by the circumference of the sphere in which it
works, or by splendor of results, but by the fidelity with
which a man administers the interests intrusted to him.

In these departments, again, there are laws having
an entirely different power and inexorableness from that
of those gotten at by generalization.   Here validity
attaches to duty, virtue, choice in the tragic conflicts
of the moral forces, in those collisions of duties which
are solved only through the power of free-will, and in
which sometimes freedom can be saved only by death.
Or are these things, too, set aside when 'the dogma of
free-will' is explained as an illusion?

Buckle does not, to be sure, go so far as to reject
that dogma of free-will because of any assumption of
its resting on the proposition that there is such a thing
as spirit or soul, and that this is a *petitio principii*.   He
does not conclude with those who explain all these
imponderables, like understanding, conscience, will, etc.,
as involuntary functions of the brain, as secretions of
I know not what gray or white matter.   Before we
believe this the great minds who thus teach must dis-
arm the suspicion that these doctrines of theirs are in
fact the secretions of their brains, and morbid secretions
at that.   But while Buckle's argument against the
presence in us of free-will is based mainly upon our
'uncertainty regarding the existence of self-consciousness,' he must either permit us to consider his own
argument, founded upon such uncertainty, as uncertain,
or else prove that he can argue without the existence
of self-consciousness, that is, of a thinking ego, and

that he has as a thought-automaton, destitute of self-consciousness, composed the work by which he intends to elevate History to the rank of a science. Nay, not 'intended,' for he denies the will along with its freedom. But some being or other must have thrown into this thinking-mill a lot of facts piled together in some way or other. The mill ground the grist, and the result, 'a swindling, tricky, subtle sophism entire,'[1] thus ground out, became the new science of History.

In spite of all this Buckle recognizes the 'progress' in History, and is unwearied in describing it as what is most truly characteristic in the life of man. This is certainly very thankworthy, but it does not accord with the main trend of his views, nor is the thought consistently carried out. If there is progress, the direction of the movement must be observed, and make itself visible to him for whose sake it exists. The method of study belonging to natural science is in a different position from this in respect to the point of view under which it apprehends phenomena. The changes which it observes it traces up to the equivalents of forces, and it sees in them only the permutations of equals and constants. Vital phenomena interest it only in so far as they repeat themselves, either periodically or morphologically. In the individual being it sees and seeks only the idea of the species or the medium of material change. Since according to its method it excludes the idea of progress, — Darwin's theory of development is the strongest proof of this, — progress not in its

---

[1] σόφισμα, κύρμα, τρίμμα, παιπάλημ' ὅλον. The quotation is from Aristophanes, *Birds*, 430, 431, where these epithets are applied to a person. — *Tr.*

knowledge, but as an element in that which it wishes to know, it has neither place nor expression for the idea of purpose, but leaves it out of account, partly degrading it to utility, thus leaving open Lessing's old question, 'what then is the utility of utility?' and partly waiving it, under forms such as the eternity of matter, evolution, etc., as a problem for other methods.

In adducing the idea of progress as a fact of the historical world, Buckle falls into a paralogism of a very striking kind. He might confess that historical investigation has not brought him to the *primum mobile*, that by the nature of empirical methods it is unattainable in this way, and that it cannot even be adequately expressed by the speech of science with its conceptions and way of thinking; but does this justify the conclusion that a *primum mobile* does not exist save as a piece of our error? Are there not various other forms of knowledge, other methods, competent, perhaps, in virtue of their nature to treat precisely the realities which the forms and methods of natural science decline and decline as a logical consequence of their point of view, and which the historical also either decline or treat inadequately? To illustrate, would there be no such thing as an æsthetic judgment because no such could be arrived at by jurists' procedure, or no legal proposition because such was sought in vain æsthetically? One who maintains that progress marks the historical world may lament that only a part of this movement peculiar to humanity is open to our view, and that we cannot descry the cause or the goal thereof, but only the fact. But will he be satisfied, and can he satisfy that deepest need of the spirit to perceive and know itself as a totality, by the circumstance that one form of empiricism shows him a riddle which another does not solve? After recognizing that a problem, a riddle, exists, will he declare it non-existent because he cannot solve it, and cannot solve it because while the enigma resides in the sense of it he wishes to see it solved as a charade, as a word-catch, or as a syllable or letter riddle? Because from the one standpoint of scientific knowledge a certain side of the total being and the universal life, namely, the metaphysical side, is invisible, being situated, by the old play upon the word, 'behind' the physical; and because from the standpoint of a knowledge differing from this the eye just grazes metaphysics a little as in perspective, must we conclude that this third side has no existence except as an illusion of ours? If we cannot take hold of light with the hands, or hear it with the ears, does it therefore not exist? Is not the fact rather that the eye is made sensitive to the sun's rays in order that by apprehending the light it may make perceptible to us what we can not seize with the hands or hear with the ears?

I pursue these questions no further, since they lie beyond the circle of thoughts in which Buckle's effort to found a scientific doctrine of History moves. The hints given will suffice to show that he has not approached the task which he proposed in the way that was necessary in order to advance it, that he appreciates neither its compass nor its dignity. And yet his task has, as it seems to me, outside of its particular significance for our studies, another which is more general, and on that account begins to engage the attention of the

scientific world. This problem appears destined to
become the middle point of the great discussion which
will mark the next important turn in the entire life of
the sciences. No one can consider the growing estrange-
ment between the exact and the speculative disciplines,
the dissidence between the materialistic and the supernatural view of the world which gapes wider day by
day, to be normal and true. These opposing contentions
demand reconciliation, and this must be worked out in
connection with Buckle's task. For the ethical world,
the world of History, which is the problem of that task,
takes part in both spheres, and it shows by every phase
of human existence and action that that contrast is no
absolute one. It is the peculiar grace of human nature,
so happily incomplete, that its ethical doings must be
at once spiritual and corporeal. Nothing human but
has place in this dissension, but lives this double life.
The opposition is reconciled each moment in order to
its renewal, renewed in order to its reconciliation. To
wish to understand the ethical or historical world is to
recognize first of all that it is not an apparition and
does not consist of a mere mutation in matter. Scientifically to transcend the false alternative between moral
and material, to reconcile the dualism of those methods
and those views of the world, each of which insists
upon ruling or denying the other, to reconcile them in
that method which applies to the ethical and historical
world, to develop them into the view of the world
which has its basis in the truth of human existence and
in the cosmos of the moral forces — that, it seems to
me, is the kernel of the problem with whose solution
we are concerned.

II. — NATURE AND HISTORY.

It is a traditional habit to apply the expression 'History' also to nature. We speak of 'Natural History,' of the 'History' of development in organic existences, of the 'History' of the globe, and so on. What else was the Okenian theory, what else is the Darwinian theory, but emphasizing the historical element, if we please so to call it, in the realm of organic nature?

Efforts are not wanting to treat History according to the laws which have been ascertained for nature, or at least according to the method built up for the natural sciences, and to establish even for the historical world the doctrine that to refer vital phenomena to physical laws is nothing less than a new conquest for science. Forms and movement in the sphere of the historical life have been characterized as 'organic developments,' and their laws given basis by means of statistical calculation. It has become customary to speak of 'natural growth' in connection with these departments, the phrase being even deemed a very special improvement.

To our science as to every other belongs the duty and the right to investigate and settle the conceptions with which it has to do. If it were to borrow these from the results of other sciences, it would be obliged to accommodate and subordinate itself to modes of view over which it has no control, perhaps to those by which it sees its own independence and right to exist called in question. It would thence perhaps receive definitions of the word 'science,' to which it would be

obliged to object.   The circle of conceptions belonging
to it our science will have to seek for itself, in its own,
that is, in an empirical manner.   It will be permitted
to attempt this because its method is the method of
understanding.   It proposes to understand terms which
language and usage in language daily employ and offer
for it to practice upon.

We find in our language the words 'nature' and
'history.'   What is meant by 'history?'   Every one
will agree that the idea of a course of time, of the
temporal, instantly connects itself with the word whenever heard.   Of eternal, that is of timeless things, so
far as we can grasp ideas of this kind, there is no
history.   They appear to us as historical only so far as
they enter into the temporal, be it through revelation,
or in their effects, or in the belief which finite minds,
minds standing under the conditions of the temporal,
have respecting them.

These minds exist 'after the image of God.'   They
are spirit set amid the conditions of finitude.   They
are countless in point of space and in ceaseless development in point of time.   The present which belongs to
them and to which they belong, is an analogue of
eternity, for eternity, which we do not know from
experience but infer from the self-consciousness of our
spiritual being, is the present as we have it, yet thought
without the limitation in which we have it, without the
change of coming and going and without the dimness
of future and past.   Human existence is Mind under
the ban of finitude, spiritual and sensuous at once and
in an inseparable manner, a contrast which is reconciled
every moment in order to its renewal, renewed in order

to its reconciliation. Our being, so long as it is itself, healthy and awake, can at no moment be merely sensuous or merely spiritual.

Another peculiarity of our spiritual nature is its power of self-vision, the ability to look into its own depths and to initiate movement within and from itself as if its outward connections were not. In thinking, believing and observing, the mind fills itself with a content that in a certain sense lies beyond the limits of finitude. Even then, though it now touches the earth with but the tips of its toes, it remains still under the ban of finitude, in the forms of conception which it has won and developed therefrom.

What occurs, now, if the spirit, in the same entirety and power, turns to the outer side of its double-formed nature? By this expression I do not refer to man's practical will and action, but to a phenomenon of his intelligence. His theoretical procedure, his investigation and discovery in practical directions, will be conditioned by his sense-life. The sensuous side of his existence does not bring to him merely as to a motionless and untroubled mirror, diversified impulses from the separate objects perceptible by sense ; but, with and through this side of his nature, as he stands in the midst of the finite objects that surround and submerge him, he is conditioned and moved by them and driven about with them, so that, in the restless dust-whirl of these restlessly changing finites, he resembles in all but a single particular the atoms which accompany him in this tumult. But the difference is after all infinite, for by virtue of his spiritual essence man has the ability to be like a fixed point in this confusion, or

at least in his soul to feel, apprehend and know himself
as such ; the ability by thinking and willing, by consciousness and self-determination, always to keep moving, in no matter how narrow a road ; the ability by
observing, estimating, and comprehending them, to
become master of things outside himself.

That the little and indigent being of man possesses
and uses this power of lordship, has always been the
riddle of contemplation. With naïve depth of view
Genesis says that when God had created all kinds of
beasts of the field and all kinds of birds of the heavens,
'he brought them unto the man to see what he would
call them : and whatsoever the man called every living
creature, that was the name thereof.' [1]   Naming was the
beginning of man's mastery over things. With the
name a sign, a spiritual counterpart was provided for
every creature or being. They were then no longer
merely in the world of outer existence ; they were
transferred to that of thought, into the mental life of
the human creature living in the midst of them.   Each
one kept the name given it, even though the form of
the manifestation corresponding to the name once im-
posed might by nutrition or exhaustion, or by repetition
in propagation, representing itself variously in various
vicissitudes, change never so much. The name was, as
it were, the permanent defining essence of the perpetually changing manifestations.   It laid hold of that
which was constant amid the change, and held it fast
as the essential thing.

In the objective, or, more correctly, the actual or external world, groups of phenomena under permanent

[1] Genesis ii: 19.

names are before us in infinite variableness, manifoldness, and differences of kind ; but the mind masters this
desolate multifariousness by taking that which is, in a
way, viz., essentially and mentally, the same, and combining it in this sameness. As to their objective or rather
their external phasis, things are simply numberless individuals in numberless combinations and separations and
in ceaseless change ; but as represented in the human
mind they stand forth fixed and classified according to
their similarities, affinities and relations. They are the
orderly signs and counterparts of the finite things chaoti-
cally flowing about us, of the confused multitude of
changing and hovering phenomena. This world of
names and ideas is to the mind the counterpart of the
world without. For us it is the truth of that world.

Thus simplifying, separating and combining, regu-
lating and subordinating, thus creating in itself a cosmos
of representations and conceptions over against the
confused world of finite realities, the human mind
makes itself by speech and thought theoretically master
of those finites amid which and the changes of which
its temporal being stands. Every human being goes
through this anew ; every one is a new beginning, a
fresh ego-creation.

Each becomes this by learning to feel and apprehend
himself as a totality within himself, by seeing, thinking,
and, so far as in him is, shaping everything that is related to him and to which he is related, however narrow
or wide this realm may be, as a closed circle about himself as its middle point. He can do this by that gift of
combining particulars according to their nature, that
restlessly working gift of simplifying and generalizing,

of separation and combination, by virtue of which he is
continually embracing wider stretches, taking them up
into his representation and, as it were, building them
into his mind. The rose, one word for countless particular attributes, he distinguishes from the pink, but,
fixing upon what is similar in the two, he calls both
flowers. He makes plants of them both, as he does of
the bushes and the grasses. Plants he sees to be quite
different from animals, yet plants and animals arise,
grow, and die in a similar manner. This life of theirs
distinguishes for him the organic world in contrast with
stone, sea, flame, and so on. He thus develops and
applies more and more comprehensive forms, more and
more general ideas.

The last and most universal of these classifications
among things perceptible by the senses, are Nature and
History. They comprehend the world of phenomena
under the two most inclusive representations ever ap-
applied, representations which have, perhaps wrongly,
been complimented by the title of intuitions *a priori*.
We are certain to embrace the totality of phenomena if
we think of them as arranged for us in space and time,
or in other words if we say Nature and History.

Obviously, whatever is in space is also in time, and
vice versa. The things of the empirical world exist
neither spatially nor temporally ; but we apprehend them
so according as the one or the other element appears
to us to preponderate, or according as we see occasion
to exalt the one or the other as the more weighty or
essential characteristic.

Of course not much is said when we have thus defined
the word 'history' and its conception, unless we are in

condition to search the notion more deeply. Space and time are the widest, that is the most empty representations of our mind. They obtain a content only in the measure in which we determine them lengthwise and crosswise, as to both succession and propinquity. This means distinguishing the particulars within them : not merely saying that they are, but what they are.

That these phenomena which we summarily embrace as History and Nature, in themselves possess other determinations and predicates than just being or being distinguished in time and space, we know by the fact that we ourselves, as to our sensuous existence, stand in the midst of them, are determined by them and are related in one way and another to them. That is, we have empirical knowledge. Without this, space and time would be to us an empty x, and the world of phenomena would remain to us a chaos. Only as we, while standing in the midst of them, separate them from ourselves, relate ourselves to them with the different sides and susceptibilities of our sensuous existence affected by now these now those exponents, and according to these exponents distinguish and compare them with each other ; only thus, in our ego, through our cognition, in our knowledge, does what exists in space and time receive wider denominations and determinations. Only thus do the empty generalities of space and time, the empty catch-alls of Nature and History develop themselves for us into a discrete content, into definite series of ideas, into particular beings existing in synthesis and succession.

Space and time are related like repose and restlessness, indolence and haste, bondage and freedom. They

are contrasted yet always bound together, inseparable
yet always wrestling with each other. For everything
is in motion. The consciousness of our life, of our
mental and sensuous existence, which, though polarized
thus in itself, is neither purely sensuous nor purely
mental nor shifting between the two, but is the living
unity of the two sides, gives us the idea of movement
and of its elements, space and time. If it were destitute
of motion the world of phenomena would be incomprehensible to us. Were we without motion in ourselves
we should not be in condition to grasp that world. By
being in motion, as ourselves are within, the world
without us permits us to understand it under the analogy of that which is going on in ourselves.

While space and time are ever united in motion,
time strives as it were to overcome indolent space in
ever new motion, and motion is all the time trying to
sink back again out of the impatience of time into the
repose of being, broadening its area by lowering its rate.
How comes it then that human observation construes
certain series of phenomena in the restless movement
of things more according to their temporal side, and
others more according to their spatial, taking the one
set as Nature, the other as History?

We certainly see constant motion and constant change
all about us ; but we separate off certain phenomena in
which the temporal element recedes, in which it appears
only transitorily, as it were, in order to sink back into
itself : phenomena which in essence repeat themselves,
in which the endless succession of time is broken up
into recurring cycles or periods of equal length. A
formation results which is 'characterized by unity, not

numerically but in nature or kind.' In such phenomena the mind lays hold of the constant, that which
abides in the midst of change, that to which motion
relates : the rule, the law, the substance, that which
fills space, etc. For it is the forms that repeat themselves here, and the immaterial character of their periodical return lowers the temporal element in their
motion to a secondary place, not indeed in relation to
their being but as regards our apprehension and understanding. This is the way in which we win for the
general notion of space its discrete content, and it is
this content which is embraced by us in the designation
'Nature.'

In other phenomena our mind emphasizes the change
in that which abides the same. It notices that here
motion results in ever new forms, formations so new
and so determinative that the material substrate on
which they appear seems like a secondary element,
while every new form is individually different from the
others, so different indeed that each, as it assumes its
place after its predecessor, is conditioned by it, grows
out of it, ideally takes it up into itself, yet when grown
out of it contains and maintains it ideally in itself. It
is a continuity, in which everything that precedes trans-
plants itself into what is later, filling it out and extending
it as 'a contribution to itself ;'[1] while the latter presents itself as a result, fulfilment, and enlargement of
the earlier. It is not the continuity of a circle that
returns into itself, of a period repeating itself, but that
of an endless succession, and this in such wise that in
every new a further new has its germ and the assurance

[1] ἐπίδοσις εἰς αὐτό.   See page 10.

of working itself out. For in every new the entire series of past forms is ideally summed up, and every one of them appears as element and temporary expression in the growing sum. In this restless succession, in this continuity advancing upon itself, the general notion of time wins its discrete content, which we designate by the expression 'History.'

Even those phenomena which we gather under the expression 'Nature' exist in individual forms, separate from each other, that is if we apprehend them also as homogeneous and similar. Out of every wheat-kernel, if it is not withdrawn from its periodic life by a different application, as germination, stalk-growth, flower, ripening of the fruit, there grows an individually different stalk, a new generation of kernels. The oaks in the same wood, though sprung each like its neighbor out of the acorns perhaps of the same maternal oak, are individually different not only in space but also in age, size, ramification, grouping of the masses of foliage, etc. We indeed perceive the differences, but they appear to us as not essential. Scientifically as practically, their individuality is immaterial to us. Among existences of this kind our mind has no special category for individuals. For this kind of individuals we have no other name than that of their species. We of course notice that they change, but in the simply periodical return of their changes they have for us no history. We indeed distinguish the individuals, but their differences show us no succession of formations advancing one upon another. We apprehend them according to space, material, the permanent in change, the indifference of self-repeating variety ; for only in these relations has our mind categories for them, and only according to these categories can we grasp and understand them, or relate ourselves to them practically or theoretically. And according to these our modes of apprehension we use and consume them, taking them for that which they are to us. We sow these wheat-kernels and care for these oaks, in order in their time to kill them and consume them as what they are to us, combustible material or farinaceous fruit. We rear these animals, in order daily to rob them of the milk provided for their young, and finally to slay them. And so on. We unweariedly observe and investigate in order to know Nature according to its materials, forces and laws, that we may apply it to our ends according to the categories under which we apprehend and comprehend it. It is for us nothing but material. In its individual manifestations we find it sealed, incomprehensible, indifferent.

And when, in grafting fruit trees, rearing animals, and crossing breeds, in order to produce nobler results, we play as it were the part of Providence, it is our cunning and calculation, not any understanding on the part of those creatures, that brings us such results. When we analyze or compound bodies chemically, or treat them physically so or so to isolate certain of their functions in order to observe these or to make them produce effects, we do not seek or find what is individually characteristic of this stone, this flame, this vibrating chord, but what is characteristic of genus or species. And when we appropriate and apply, æsthetically, for instance, the temporary forms which the animal or the plant world or the landscape offers us, we well know that it is not the individuality of this piece of the

earth's surface, of this tree or animal, which we wish
understood and represented thereby ; but that we put
something into them which is not in them, something
quite remote from them, in fact, so that these items of
nature serve us only as expressions of our feeling or
thought, we, so to speak, anthropomorphising them ; as
in Dante's Purgatory the loathsome picture of lust becomes under the passionate glance of the man surveying
it in desire, a woman blooming in beauty.

Also in the moral world, in the realm of those realities which we call History, there are elements which
can be measured, weighed and calculated. But these
material conditions by no means exhaust the life of the
moral world, or suffice to explain it ; and whoever
thinks that he can explain it in this manner overlooks
or denies that which is here essential. The sexual impulse does not exhaust or explain the moral might of
marriage. Common remembrance of common experiences, possession of common hopes and cares, losses and
successes, renew again even for couples who are growing
old, the warmth of their first bliss. For them their marriage has a history. In this history its moral might was
founded for them, and it is justified and fulfilled in and
by the same.

In the moral universe there is certainly nothing
which may not be subject directly or indirectly to material conditions, though the material conditions are not
the only ones operative or determinative in this realm.
The nobility of our moral being consists in the fact that
it does not in any way deny or falsely estimate its envi-
ronment, but rather in fact illuminates and spiritualizes
this. It is thus that the contact of minds in their work

upon and with one another, in their restless impulse to shape things and to understand and be understood, develops this marvellous stratum of spiritual being which enswathes our globe, forever touching the natural world and yet free from it.   Its elements are representations, thoughts, passions, mistakes, guilt and the like.

It does not imply too light an estimate of the moral world to lay it down that this restlessly flowing and swelling stratum of spiritual existence is the habitat and ground of its formations, the plastic mass, so to speak, where they originate.   Such formations are certainly none the less realities, or of less power objectively, because they essentially live only in the souls, hearts, knowledge, and consciences of human beings, and employ the body and things of a bodily kind merely as their expressions, bearing their impress.   True, they can be perceived, understood, and investigated only in these expressions and impressions ; but they do not exist merely that the historical method may be applied to them.   They can be scientifically surveyed from still other points of view than the historical.   They are open to this, for what they are they have become, and to make out the development of things from their developed forms, and their developed forms from their development is the nature of the historical method.

We offer, in conclusion, one more remark to parry objections.   No one thinks of contesting the application to physics of the name of science, or of doubting the scientific results of physical research, although the science is not nature, but only a manner of observing nature.   No one objects to mathematics on the ground that its whole proud structure stands only within the

knowing mind.   Our shrewd mother tongue forms from
the participle of the word 'to know' (*wissen*) its
descriptive for that which is certain (*gewiss*).   It does
not name the outer and so-called objective being of
things 'certain,' but beings and occurrences considered
as 'known.'   Not what addresses us as sensuously
perceptible is 'true,' according to our language.   No
material thing presents itself to us as 'true,' but we
'take it true'[1] and make it certain by means of our
knowledge.

'*Our* perception,' '*our* knowledge' : here would lurk
the most dubious subjectivism, were the human world
composed of atoms, each filling its span of space and
time, and without any connection from beginning to end ;
or of atomic men as exemplified by the old philosopher's
plucked cock, and by the view of man which modern
radicalism takes as the starting point of its human
rights, and modern materialism and nihilism for the
basis of their 'sociology.'   The individual as such
could not even be born, to say nothing of being cared
for, brought up, and developed into a human adult.
From the moment of his birth, and even of his conception, he has place in the moral partnerships, this
family, this nation, State, faith or unfaith, etc., and it
is from and through them that he originally receives
whatever he is and has, whether of bodily or of spiritual
fortune.

It is clear that the scepticism of these views does not
go to controvert the reality of the natural world, still

---

[1] *Wahrnehmen*, literally 'to take as true' (*wahr*, 'true,' and
nehmen, 'take,') is in German psychology the technical word denot-
ing 'to perceive.' — *Tr*.

less the actuality of the historical or moral formations. To us nature is not a 'phantom of the brain.' Even less is the moral world the threadbare 'affirmation of the will to live.' Practically we live and act in the confident self-feeling of our ego-hood, and also in the direct apprehension of the outer totality in the midst of which we stand. These are the two elements which result from the character of our being, spiritual and sensuous at once.

On this immediate certainty with which we cognize ourselves and the world, on this belief, however high or low the expression we have arrived at for its ultimate ground or its highest end, is based our human existence and activity. This immediate reality we possess, and we go on to search for and work out the truth beneath it, which grows and deepens as we search and work. In the poverty of our ego-hood and ego-development — and this is present and irrepressible with our first spoken word — lies the pressure upon us to bring to our consciousness what is perceived and believed, to comprehend it, to free it as it were from the umbilical cord which attaches it to the immediate realities, and arrange it in order among the categories of our thinking. These categories are related to the totality of the actual things which we immediately perceive, including our ego-hood, as the polygon is to the circle. Never so many-sided and similar to a circle, the polygon remains angular and bounded by straight lines, circle and polygon never ceasing to be mutually incommensurable.

It is the mistaken pride of the human mind to bolster the circles of what it directly apprehends upon its own angular constructions as their norm or confirmation, while in fact these constructions are only effort upon effort gradually to trace a line outside those circles. We deny the spherical lines of faith because our thought can not exhaust them with its right-lined figures, any more than that boy of Augustine's, eagerly as he might bail with his shell, could dry the hole which he had dug on the shore, when the sea was always ready to pour over into it.

III. — ART AND METHOD.

Poetry was composed before poetics arose, as people talked before there were grammar and rhetoric. Practical needs had taught men to mix and analyze materials and to apply the powers of nature to human purposes, before chemistry and physics had methodically investigated nature and expressed its laws in scientific form.

Recollections also belong to humanity's deepest nature and needs. However narrow or wide the circles which they may embrace, they are never in any wise wanting to men. In the highest degree personal as they at first appear, they yet form a bond between the souls which meet in them. No human community is without them. Each possesses in its previous life and history the image of its being, a common possession of all participants, which makes their relationship so much the firmer and more intimate.

We can believe that the memories of highly gifted peoples are embellished in their sagas, and become types for the expression of the ideals to which the spirit of the people is directed. We can suppose also that their faith gets for them its basis in the form of sacred stories,

which present the contents of it to the eye as actual
occurrences, and that such myths grow along with the
sagas. But when this restlessly living fusion, finally
satiated, comes to an end in the form of great epics,
myths will no longer belong to the naïve faith alone.

The earliest history, that of the Greeks, began with
the collection and sifting of such myths and sagas.
Theirs were the earliest efforts to bring into this pri-
meval forest of traditions order, connection, agreement,
a chronological system, the first attempts at real investigation. From the Greeks dates the continuity of the
sciences. Almost all of these which busy men's minds
to-day had their beginnings in Greece. Particularly
the field which has been well designated as that of the
moral sciences was tilled by them with predilection.
But they have no treatise on the Principles of History,
no 'historics,' to accompany their ethics, politics, eco-
nomics, etc.

After geniuses had historically described the age of
Marathon and the age of Pericles, Thucydides being
the last member of the galaxy, it was left to Isokrates
and not to Aristotle to found an historical school. This
fact drew history into paths from which Polybius vainly
exerted himself to bring it back. It became, and with
the Romans it remained, so far as philology did not get
possession of it, a part of rhetoric or *belles lettres*.
Between the two, philology and rhetoric, historical
sketches for practical purposes, including encyclopedias
and school books, gradually sank to the most miserable
dryness.

We come to the middle age. Its historical work is
even less likely to betray any new impulses toward

scientific thought than is that of declining antiquity, unless we except the sense for theological construction which the middle age here and there exhibits. This judgment is true, in spite of the fact that an occasional historian in the times of the Carolingians and the Ottos sought his model of style among the ancients and tricked out his heroes with their rhetorical flourishes.

As the middle age drew to a close, the renewed strife against the papacy and the hierarchy seized upon historical investigation as a weapon, and the researches in regard to the alleged donation of Constantine were followed stroke after stroke by historico-critical attacks upon the false traditions, the anti-scriptural institutions, and the canonical assumptions of the Church. Even then, however, in these important scientific onsets, rhetoric again and speedily got the upper hand of history. This occurred first in Germany. The last magnificent attempt on the German side, that of Sebastian Franck, scientifically to collate the knowledge and practice which had been won, was drowned by the din of the brawl, so soon grown dogmatic, between the creeds.

Only after the natural sciences, sure and conscious of their way, had established their method and thereby made a new beginning in scientific thought, did the notion emerge of finding a methodical side even for the 'methodless matter'[1] of History. To the time of Galileo and Bacon belongs Jean Bodin ; to that of Huygens and Newton, Pufendorff and also Leibnitz, the thinker, who broke paths in all directions at once. Then the English Illumination, if it is permitted thus to name the period of the so-called deists, took up this question. To

[1] $\dot{\alpha}\mu\dot{\epsilon}\theta o\delta o\varsigma$ $\ddot{\upsilon}\lambda\eta.$ See page 62.

its representations was due the first effort to divide our science according to its problems or departments. They spoke of the History of the World, the History of Humanity, Universal History, the History of States, of peoples, and so on. Voltaire, the pupil and continuator of this English tendency, contributed to it the unclear designation '*philosophie de l' histoire.*' The Göttingen historical school developed a kind of system among the newly created sciences and associate sciences in their field, and began to infuse its spirit even into branches but remotely connected with History. More than one of the great poets and thinkers of our nation went deep into the theoretical question of historical certitude ; and there developed in historical labor and investigation itself a habit of sharp and certain criticism, which produced entirely new and surprising results in every realm of History where it was applied. In this historical criticism the German nation has ever since Niebuhr outstripped all others ; and the style or technique of investigation maintained in the splendid labors of German *savans* seemed to need only expression in general and theoretical propositions in order to constitute the historical method.

To be sure, the great public was not at once served by this application of our historical toil. It wished to read, not to study, and complained that we set before it the process of preparing food instead of the food itself. It called the German method in history pedantic, exclusive, unenjoyable. How much more agreeable to read were Macaulay's Essays than these learned and tiresome investigations ! How the accounts of the French Revolution in Thiers's splendid delineation took! In this way it came to pass that not only German historical taste but German historical judgment, and consequently in no slight degree also German political judgment, being all formed and guided for three or four centuries by the foreign style of making History, were dominated by the rhetorical superiority of other nations.

This is not all. While such rhetorical art takes weighty and tremendous events, with the difficult entanglements in which they are usually wrought out or at least prepared for, and sadly metamorphoses them, as it depicts the horror of men's unchained passions and fanatic persecutions, the false representation, though discordant enough artistically, yet has a thrilling and dramatic effect when read. Composition is certain to be so much the more comprehensible and persuasive for being of that kind. It is able to make even the less intelligent reader acquainted with things which in their actual course demanded from the contemporary who wished to understand them in never so moderate a degree, a thousand points of previous knowledge, besides much experience and a calm and collected judgment. Historical art knows how in the most felicitous manner to avoid all this, so that the attentive reader, when he has perused his Thiers or Macaulay to the end, is permitted to believe himself the richer by the great experiences of the revolutions, party-wars, and constitutional developments of which they treat. 'Experiences,' forsooth! when they lack the best of what makes experiences fruitful, the earnestness of actual men hard at work, responsibility for irrevocable decisions, the sacrifice which even victory demands, the failure which treads under foot the most righteous cause! The art of the historian lifts the reader above thought of any such side issues. It fills his fancy with representations and views which embrace but the splendidly illuminated tips of the broad, hard, tediously slow reality. It persuades him that these sum up all the particular events and constitute the truth of the realities not dwelt upon. It helps in its way the limitless influence of public opinion, leading people to measure the reality according to their ideas and to call upon reality to form or transform itself accordingly. Readers demand this the more impatiently the easier custom has made it for them to think of such a reversal of things. We Germans too already boast an historical literature answering the popular need. Among us as elsewhere the insight is attained or the confession made that 'History is at once art and science.' At the same time the question of method, which is what we are concerned with here, is falling into obscurity anew.

What then, in works of an historical kind, is the mutual relation between art and science? For instance, is the fact that History is marked by 'criticism and learning' enough to give it a scientific character? Is that incumbent on art which the historian ought in any event to do? Should the historian's studies actually have no other aim than that he may write a few books? Should they have no application but to entertain by instructing and to instruct by entertaining?

History is the only science enjoying the ambiguous fortune of being required to be at the same time an art, a fortune which, in spite of Platonic dialogues, not even philosophy shares with it. It would not be without interest to inquire the reason for this peculiarity of History.

We, however, pass to another side of the question. In artistic labors, according to an old manner of expression, technique and Muses' work go hand in hand. It belongs to the nature of art that its productions make you forget the defects which inhere in its means of expression. Art can do this in proportion as the idea which it wishes to bring out in given forms, upon such and such materials, and with this technique, vivifies and illumines all these. What is created in such a manner is a totality, a world in itself. Muses' work has the power to make the observer or hearer fully and exclusively receive and feel in a given expression what that work was meant to express.

It is different with the sciences. Particularly the empirical ones have no more imperative duty than to make clear the gaps which are based in the objects of their search; to control the errors which arise out of their technique ; to inquire the scope of their methods, recognizing that they can give right results only within the limits essentially pertaining to them.

Perhaps the greatest service of the critical school in History, at least the one most important in respect to method, is to have given rise to the insight that the groundwork of our studies is the examination of the 'sources' from which we draw. In this way the relation of History to past events is placed at the point which yields a scientific rule. This critical view that past events lie before us no longer directly, but only in a mediate manner, that we can not restore them 'objectively,' but can only frame out of the 'sources' a

more or less subjective apprehension, view, or copy of
them, that the apprehensions and views thus attainable
and won are all that it is possible for us to know of the
past, that thus 'History' exists not outwardly and as
a reality, but only as thus mediated, studied out, and
known, — this, so it seems, must be our point of departure if we will cease to 'naturalize' in history.

What is before us for investigation is not past events
as such, but partly remnants of them, partly ideas of
them.   The remnants are such only for historical consideration.   They stand as wholes and on their own
account in the midst of this present, many of them,
fragmentary and widowed as they are, instantly remind-
ing us that they were once different, more alive and
important than now ; others transformed and still in
living and practical application ; others changed almost
beyond recognition and fused in the being and life of
the present.   The present itself is nothing else but the
sum of all the remnants and products of the past.
Furthermore, views of what was and happened are not
always from contemporaries, those acquainted with the
facts, or impartial witnesses, but often views of views,
at third or fourth hand.   And even when contemporaries
tell what happened in their time, how much did they
personally see and hear of what they relate ?   One's
own eye-sight and hearing embrace after all but a part,
a side, a tendency of the occurrences.   And so on.

In point of method the character of these two kinds
of materials is so extraordinarily different that one does
well to keep them separate even in technical nomencla-
ture ; and it behooves such as wish their writings to be
sources to name their sources even when in most respects

they are like the other remnants, being literary remains of the time in which they arose.

The now usual method or technique of historical investigation was developed from the study of times which have transmitted, at least for political history, nothing or little but the sort of views above characterized, from more or less contemporary narrators. Much for which we should like to seek and inquire, these accounts do not touch at all. To the question how our emperors when they crossed the Alps on their journeys to Rome cared for thousands of men and horses, to the question in what form the commerce of the Mediterranean was carried on after the revolution which Alexander the Great effected over all Asia, the sources give us no information.

How superficial, how unreliable our knowledge of earlier times is, how necessarily fragmentary and limited to particular points the view which we can now gather therefrom, we become conscious even when we study times from which the archives offer us something more than the 'original documents' of closed public law cases ; giving us diplomatic reports, reports of administrative authorities and state papers of all kinds. And further, how vividly prominent in such study is the difference between the ' views ' of the foreign ambassadors or of the domestic authorities, and the remains that survive of the actual course of diplomacy, the deliberations back and forth, the protocols of the negotiations, and so on. Certainly these state documents do not as a rule, like those narrations, lay before us an already formed idea of the case, a preliminary historical picture of what had just happened.

They are remnants of that which happened ; they are pieces of the transaction and of the course it pursued, which still lie directly before our eyes. And if I may give the expression so wide an application, it is as a 'transaction,' in the broad maze of the present, conditioned and conditioning in a thousand ways, that those events come to pass which we afterwards apprehend successively as History. We thus look at them in a quite different way from that in which they occurred, and which they had in the wishes and deeds of those who enacted them. So it is not a paradox to ask how History (*Geschichte*) comes out of transactions (*Geschäften*), and what it is which with this transfer into another medium, as it were, is added or lost.

I may be permitted to offer a single remark in conclusion. I have in another place sought to refute the contention made against our science by those who view the method of natural science as the only scientific one, and who think that History must be raised to the rank of a science through the application of that method. Just as if in the realm of the historical, that is, of the moral life, only analogy were worthy of regard and not also anomaly, the individual, free-will, responsibility, genius. As if it were not a scientific task to seek ways of investigation, of verification, of understanding for the movements and effects of human freedom and of personal peculiarities, however high or low the estimate which may be placed upon them.

We certainly possess immediately and in subjective certainty, an understanding of human things, of every expression and impression of man's creation or behavior which is perceptible to us, so far as it is perceptible.   What we have to do is to find methods, in order to secure objective rules and control for this immediate and subjective grasp of events, especially as we now have before us, to represent the past, only the views of others or fragments of that which once existed.   We need to ground, sound and justify our subjective knowledge.   Only this seems able to assert itself as the sense of the historical objectivity so often named.

We are to discover methods.   There is need of different ones for different problems, and often a combination of several is required for the solution of one problem. So long as History was believed to be essentially political history, and the task of the historian was just to recount in new presentation and connection what had been transmitted about revolutions, wars, state events, etc., it might suffice to take for use from the best sources, which had perhaps been critically authenticated as the best, the material to be wrought into a book, a lecture, or the like.   But since the insight has been awakened that also the arts, jural formations, everything of human creation, all the formations characterizing the moral world, can and must be investigated in order to deduce that which is from that which was, demands of a very different kind are made upon our science.   It has to investigate formations according to their historical connection, formations of which perhaps only individual remnants are preserved, to open fields hitherto not considered or treated as historical, least of all by those who lived in the midst of them.   Thus questions are pressing upon History from all sides, questions touching things for the most part incomparably weightier than the often very superficial and accidental accounts which have hitherto passed for History. Is investigation to lay down its arms here?

When we enter a collection of Egyptian antiquities, we have at once the subjective view of their wonderful ancientness, and the accompanying strange impression; but at least in certain directions we can by investigation come to more positive results. Here are these syenites, hewn and polished. Here are these colors, these woven fabrics. What tools, what metals were required to work such hard stone? What mechanical contrivances were needed to raise such masses out of the quarry and put them aboard ship? How were these colors prepared chemically? Out of what materials are these fabrics made and whence did they come? In the way of such technological interpretation of remains, facts are made out which in numerous and important directions fill up our meagre tradition concerning ancient Egypt; and these facts possess a certainty so much the greater for the indirectness of the manner in which they were deduced.

Many think it the part of criticism, touching, for instance, the constitution of ancient Rome or Athens before the Persian wars, to allow only that to pass as good history which is explicitly transmitted and attested. The reader's fancy will not fail to combine these scanty notices and thus to fill them out into a picture; only, this filling out is commonly a play of the fancy, and the picture more or less artificial. Is it not possible to find methods which will regulate the process of such filling out, and give it a foundation? In the pragmatic nature exhibited by things of this kind — and writers should leave off misapprehending Polybius's expression 'pragmatic' — lie elements, conditions, necessities, traces of which, provided we look more sharply, may perhaps be re-recognized in what still lies before us. The hypothetical line which enabled us to trace that pragmatic nature of things then confirms itself, since this or that fragment exactly fits into it.

When it was necessary to work out the history of art during the times of Raphael and Dürer, not much advance could be made with the 'sources' and the criticism of sources, although in Vasari and others, at least for the Italian masters, was found just the external information that was desired. In their works and those of their German contemporaries, however, was found something entirely different, exactly the material for investigation, though confessedly of a nature which required in the investigator who was to derive exact results from it, an outfit of an especial kind. He was obliged to know the technique of painting, in order to distinguish that of the different artists, the tint of each one's tone, his chiaroscuro, his brush-stroke. He was obliged to be sure how Albrecht Dürer's eye envisaged the human form, else he could not show whether a given crucifix was from his hand. In order finally to decide whether this or that important portrait head was by Leonardo da Vinci or Holbein, he had to bring to his work, so to speak, a learned apparatus of etchings, hand sketches, etc. He must be familiar with the mode of looking at things in that age, the range of its general knowledge, its common convictions, ecclesiastical and profane, its local and daily history, that he might be able rightly to interpret what was presented

in the works of art or in things related thereto. He
was called upon not only æsthetically to feel but per-
suasively to point out the artist's deeper or more superficial view or intention.

The same in all other departments. Only the deep
and many sided technical and special knowledge, according as it is art, law, commerce, agriculture, or the
State and politics that is to be historically investigated,
will put the investigator in condition to ascertain the
methods demanded for the given case, and to work
with them.   Just so new methods are continually
found out in the natural sciences to unlock dumb
nature's mysteries.

All such methods which come into play in the realm
of historical studies move within the same periphery
and have the same determining centre.   To unite them
in their common thought, to develop their system and
their theory, and so to establish, not the laws of objective History but the laws of historical investigation and
knowledge, — this is the task of *Historik*.

INDEX.